BEING
BLACK N BLUE

THIRTY-FIVE YEARS IN BLUE
A Black LAPD Veteran's Stories of Triumph and
Tragedies—the Real Deal

Michael Brox

Published and Distributed By
MAB True Enterprises LLC
Sylmar, CA 91342

Packaging/Consulting
Professional Publishing House
1425 W. Manchester Ave. Ste. B
Los Angeles, California 90047
323-750-3592
Email: professionalpublishinghouse@yahoo.com
www.professionalpublishinghouse.com

Cover design: TWA Solutions
First printing June 2018
978-0-692-12634-9
10987654321

Dedications

I dedicate this book and the work that made it possible to my mother, Odessa Brox. As an author, she inspired me in so many different ways. A single parent of several children, she worked tirelessly to provide for her family, kept God in her heart first, and a .22 caliber pistol second in her purse.

She was the world to me. We did not always agree, but the respect I had for her was unmatched. Mommy, I know you would not have approved of the language or some of my behavior illustrated on these pages, but I know you would understand.

My mother most certainly would have been proud of my growth as a strong black man. She would be pleased with my work in our community. She would be happy with my strength to endure when things went terribly wrong. Overall, she would be thankful to God that I was safe and I could stand up, be a man, and care for my family. I love you, Mommy. Rest in peace.

To my family...

Shirlye, my wife of thirty-three years, it has been a great ride. A bit bumpy at times, but know I APPRECIATE you. I don't know if I would have made it through this LAPD and life journey without you.

My daughters: Camille, Courtney, and Calynne—you three have made this old man so proud. I am pleased beyond words with each one of your life directions. Thank you for supporting me and being honest and open. Keep family first and love each other 'til the wheels fall off.

To my sisters: Linda Kay (Wafer), Vanessa, Vicky, and Gradietta (Cookie)

To my brothers: Reginald (Reggie, Big Red, or "the Big Man") and Jamal (Jake, Snake)

I love you all. You all have been my protectors, my audience, and my supporters all my life. Thanks!

A special thanks to you, Reggie, man! You have been like a father to me all my life. You have and still are my teacher, my manly and father example. You scolded me when I needed it, you beat me up when I deserved it, and praised me when it was worthy. I love you, man!

Acknowledgments

There is one person who has helped me so much and she is my friend Tracy Lemon (Shotlow). Girl, if it had not been for those late night edits with you, Brandi, Brittany, and the use of your household technology, this most likely would have failed.

Tracy, for so many years, you have been like a sister. You have been there for me when tears were in my eyes, anger in my heart, and joy in my spirit. Your advice, support, and conversation are second to none. I love you for that and so much more.

Thank you, my dear lifelong friend.

Table of Contents

PREFACE

Something Is Not Right!

A foot search along the Harbor Freeway (Interstate 110) embankment, covered by tall, thick trees, trash, dirt, rodents and a large carcass, perhaps a dog rotting for weeks, and the smell that was almost unbearable, yet we continue to search. Even in daylight, it was difficult to see beyond a few feet, the footing was difficult as the ground was loose dirt, leaves, and rolling branches from dying scrubs. The slope at about a forty-five-degree angle, yet several uniformed officers from 77th Street Division and I, a brand new rookie, along with several other officers from neighboring divisions, pressed on to find a suspected car thief last seen fleeing a stolen car ditched after a chase and crash on the freeway.

I heard several white officers alerting the suspect to our presence.

"We're coming to get you, nigger."

At twenty-one years young and scared to death, I was hoping the suspect did not come out and shoot me. I kept my game face on.

An officer found him buried, trying to hide and avoid capture. But, as I would learn daily, that is not the only reason young, black men, boys, and women hide from Los Angeles Police Department (LAPD) officers.

The officers beat, stomped, kicked, and hit that young man with wooden batons until he was near unconsciousness. Lesson: don't hide from the POLICE.

As most young boys, we played cops and robbers, watched television shows; all we knew were the police drove cars fast, chased the bad guys, shot guns, and wore a cool uniform.

As a young, black man from a single-parent household, I had dreams of playing professional baseball and being a policeman or fireman.

Several area coaches told my mother and me I had the makings of a very good baseball player. She, however, had church and serving the Lord on her mind. So, the opportunities of being a part of advanced training and a more competitive baseball program in Long Beach, California, was out of the question; money and weekend travel shattered that dream.

"As for me and my house, we are going to serve the Lord," she said. So, sports came after going to church. She never allowed me to miss many church services.

My mother was the biggest influence on me as a young man. She cared for me while I was sick, and scolded me (with a beating) when I screwed up and disobeyed the rules of her house. She praised and supported her children when we did the right things. I love my mommy and miss her every single day. I love you, Odessa Brox. My mother passed in May 2011. Rest in peace and in heaven.

In 1968, my family escaped the Pueblo Housing Projects of Los Angeles, and arrived in the City of Gardena, California. We were the first black family to move into the neighborhood. Our street and surrounding neighbors in Gardena were middle income, two-parent households. The ethnic makeup was majority white with a splash of Asian families.

Within two years, white and Asian families had moved out of the neighborhood. Increasingly, blacks moved into the area with a few Hispanic families here and there.

I was familiar with all the kids within a few years of my age. We attended the same schools and grew up together. Some went the way of achievement and others chose a life of jail and foolishness.

The area police and sheriff's departments were very unfair to us as young, black boys and teenagers. We held no affiliation with gangs, but law enforcement officers did not care.

When I was eleven years old, I recall a group of us—my older brother, three others, and I—were walking on Vermont Avenue on a summer afternoon, on our way to Rosecrans Park in Gardena. We walked to Rosecrans because our parents were working or taking care of the house. The community parks offered kids in the area a chance to take part in sports and activities sponsored by cities and managed by caring adults that worked to enhance the area youth experience.

It was routine for Gardena Police to fuck with us for no other reason than we were black kids, walking on the sidewalk. Asking questions like, "Where are you boys going?" My brother was the oldest and spoke up for our group, only to hear, "Turn around and go back home." If he, or any of us, said anything in opposition or asked questions, their response would often be, "What the fuck did you say, boy?" They would pull out their nightsticks, puff up, and say things like, "Take your black ass home or you can go to jail for resisting an officer."

This was a common occurrence. Gardena Police, Compton Police, Hawthorne Police, the Sheriff's Department, and LAPD were notorious for being violent and unfair toward young, black men within and around Los Angeles. It was so bad, that most churches, community parks, and elders taught us how to stay alive during encounters with the police.

CHAPTER ONE

We Don't Bang!

One summer day, my friend "Donut" and I were waiting for a bus to arrive to take us to summer school.

A Payback Crip strolled up on us. I have known this cat since the 5th grade, a book-smart brother who chose the street and gang life. We all were from the same neighborhood who's tag was, "The Payback."

"We finna squab wit' dem S-Guns. You down, Brox?" he asked me.

The S-Gun, Shotgun Crips lived just west of our neighborhood.

I responded, "Naw, man, you know I don't gang bang!"

Before I knew it, these cats from "the gun" were everywhere; people fighting, screaming, cussing, and then someone produced a rifle.

I saw the bus heading our way. I ran toward it, as shots rang out, a bullet struck someone. The bus driver tried to change lanes. I ran into the street, banging on the doors, as it continued slowly moving. He finally opened the door.

Donut and I jumped into the bus, crawled on the floor, and yelled to the driver, "Floor it, man! Get us out of here."

The *Gardena Valley News* reported that a gang fight at the corner of Vermont Avenue and 135th Street ended in the shooting death of one youth and injuries to several others. We escaped. Later that same school year at Gardena High School, during lunch period with my two friends, a lifelong friend from our neighborhood, who was football player (not a gang member) came over to us. He told us over the weekend that this guy who was a Shotgun Crip had beaten up his younger brother at a party and took his leather jacket or hat or something.

He asked us to go with him because he wanted to whoop this guy's ass. The Crip went to Gardena, too. He wanted us to make sure nobody jumped into the fight.

Okay, why not! *Dummy.* We all walked over to this brother; he was big.

Perhaps we should rethink this, I thought.

One of our friends yelled, "Man, don't talk, still on this mother fucker!"

Well, our friend was not much of a street guy. It looked like this was his first street fight, so he hit this guy in his stomach. That did not work well. The fight was on. This Crip was kicking my friend's ass. I heard, "Help me!" He asked us to keep others from jumping in. He said nothing about helping him fight.

Somebody hit me in the ear. I turned around and saw a light-skinned, skinny punk I knew. He was a wannabe gangster. I grabbed his shirt with my left hand and threw punches on this fucker as if my life depended on it. We ended up on the ground, rolling in the ivy. I was getting stomped, I guess by his gang buddies. It did not matter; he was under me, as long as he was getting the business from me. Security came to his rescue.

They pulled me off him. I had grass and leaves in my 'fro (had just gotten a blowout), snails in my pocket, tree branches sticking out my ass. "Where's my shoe?"

The school suspended me. Only thing that concerned me about the suspension was my mother would find out.

The next day, my mother said, "Get up and go to school."

"I got suspended from school, Momma."

She gave me a beating at home for being stupid. That was not a good week.

Our high school basketball team made the 1978 City Playoffs. I, along with other Gardena High School's athletes, traveled to Crenshaw High School for a first-round playoff, though we were not on the basketball team.

Dressed in our letterman jackets and Gardena Mohican beanies, we were showing off our athletic achievements. Despite our antics in the stands, our team got the daylights beaten out of them. That was not the end.

A short, pimp-looking, ponytail wearing, shit-talking gangster came to the stands where we sat during the game. "Y'all talking all that shit, now what?" Time to go!

The biggest fight broke out. I had driven there. I took off running, with Ponytail and some other dudes chasing my boys and me. We made it to my car, a shiny new Toyota Corolla.

A loud crash alerted us to the back window being shattered. I drove out of that parking lot as fast as I could. We made it to

Crenshaw Boulevard. I later found out that Ponytail would later become Ice-T. I should go to one of his movie sets and tell him he owes me $80.00 for my broken care window.

High school was three years during the '70s. I played junior varsity baseball and ran track. I was small but very good. I was batting an average of 304. Had speed on the bases and a good glove. I needed to get my arm stronger. The varsity coach from Banning High School watched me play as I grew up. During my first high school season, he asked me to transfer to Banning to be a part of their varsity team. I turned him down. I was a Mohican. Biggest mistake I made in high school. I never played on Gardena's varsity team. They were a shitty team anyway—no development, no conditioning—not a real program. They chose players based on the honorary system—if their brothers or other family members played on the team. It was the same thing with football. Good on the gridiron, I played with and against the same cats on the football teams at Gardena. Some of them asked, "Why are you not playing?" During our first Bee Football tryouts, I was one of the fastest clocked in the forty-yard dash—4.56. That was flying back then. I always led one of the running drills. One coach told me I was too skinny and needed to gain weight. He was always making comments on my size, even though I was killing in running and skill drills. So, I let it get the best of me and I quit. I regret it to this day.

This was the start and end of a dream. It quickly turned into a nightmare of a trend becoming a "quitter" for several years and different challenges in my life.

The varsity coach told me to play another year of junior varsity and then play one year at the varsity level. I saw less talented white guys as freshman on the varsity team and some being moved up while I, and other talented brothers, was left behind. So, I quit high school baseball.

I ran one of the fastest forty-yard dash times for the Bee football team. But, I quit. Went onto junior college and played on their team. After one season of sitting on the bench behind returning players, I quit.

I was in college taking a few classes, working two jobs as a grocery clerk, and at a rental car company, but my paychecks were not enough to pay rent, my $76.00 a month car note, and other expenses, including school.

I attended a job fair on campus and, despite the treatment my young friends and me received from the police during my young and teen years, I applied for the Los Angeles Fire Department, LAPD, Gardena Police Department, and Culver City Police Department. I was too short to work for Gardena Police Department (yeah, right) and then LAPD called and the process started. Determined to make a difference, treat people fair, help those in need, and put jackass criminals in jail, I had no idea what I was getting myself into.

I met with my background investigator, a tall thin white guy, sort of young looking, no mustache, not sharply dressed, but with a wrinkled shirt and tie, sport coat that resembled a potato sack and carried a visible tiny revolver in a shoulder holster. Every time I met with him, he seemed to have on the same clothes.

During the process, I gave him all the places I lived, schools I attended, and references he asked for. I was working and in school, but I had a run in with Hawthorne Police Department that resulted in a bullshit, felony arrest. That arrest was later dismissed and my background investigator found that it would not impact me in the hiring process.

However, what was a deep concern for him was my driving record and that I told him I did not drink alcohol, smoke weed or any other drugs.

He told me he could not believe a young, black man, who grew up in the projects, played sports at local parks and from a single parent home, did not get high or drink alcohol.

"You may be disqualified just for lying," I remembered him saying.

Wow! My only response to him was to ask *any* of my references, which included neighbors, coaches, teachers, and church members, if they have known me to partake in any of the aforementioned behaviors. I owned up to my driving history. I belonged to a street-racing club, often received tickets, and ran from the police several times, but only caught once and that was because I ran out of gas.

He did his background check and could not confirm his beliefs. He *still* did not believe I did not do drugs or alcohol.

He asked me if I would take a polygraph test. I told him I would, but only if any of the white candidates were taking polygraph exams, too. A white friend went through the process and they did not offer him to take a polygraph test. Though, they fired him during the academy for drugs, alcohol abuse, and wife beating.

My background investigator never mentioned a polygraph again, and recommended me for hire. I breezed through all other testing and entered the academy with LAPD Recruit class 7/81 (July 27, 1981).

CHAPTER TWO

The Beginning of My Awakening

Monday through Friday from 7:00 a.m. to 5:00 p.m., for six months of intense academic, physical training and self-defense, tactics and situational simulations, our class of eighty plus young and older men, women, and a few black recruits were to work together to graduate.

It was to be a bond of brotherhood, the family of blue and willingness to pull each other along as a group with one goal—to become a member of the LAPD to protect and serve. Some came in with their own agenda and some with ulterior motives. Some discovered during training, others slipped through. I had this in my heart. It was the first time I would not quit, despite the obstacles during training, but the one who I thought slipped through pushed me to the limit.

At the Academy, I was one of the fastest runners with above average endurance and appointed to be a road guard, one who ran ahead of the class during street runs and often called to double back to help the slower runners catch up and then get back to the front of the pack. So, I often ran longer distances as the group, which I didn't mind.

One very hot day during a difficult run, I received the order. "Brox, get back and bring up the turtle squad." Turtle squad was a name given to the slower members of the class. I ran to greet a group of women and one guy, who had race issues and was from some one-horse town in the middle of nowhere USA.

I was pushing them. "Come on, let's go! Pick it up! You can do it!" I put my hands on the back of a couple women who were struggling to climb this hill, using my legs, speed, and endurance to help my LAPD recruit family make it. I offered this guy my hand.

"Fuck you," he said.

Okay, I thought, and I went up the hill with those that needed and accepted help.

In the men's locker room, I asked this guy what were the issues.

"Don't you ever touch me, nigger."

Shocked, I retaliated and the fight was on. Punching and wrestling in nothing but our underwear, the fight seemed to last for a long time, but other members of the class broke it up rather quickly. The brothers stood by me and the white guys stood by him. He drew the line in the sand and the support seemed endangered.

Someone ratted. Yes, we had a snitch in our group. A drill instructor called the white guy and me into his office and chastised me up and down for being thin-skinned.

"What are you going to do, fight everyone that calls you out of your name? People out there hate us and the badge you wear; you cannot fight everyone in the street that hates you."

I responded with respect and a simple question. "Sir, I understand, but to be called a nigger by someone who is supposed to be professional and supposed to represent LAPD; is that what I am supposed to accept?"

"Don't worry about anyone but yourself. Don't be so thin-skinned. You will hear and see worse than that if you graduate from my academy."

I guess LAPD's Training Division accepted being a racist and to use such an offensive term. He was right. I had to worry about myself. He could see into the future.

I recall in some of our situation simulations and during our physical training, the verbal scenarios (what if's) used by some (a lot) of the instructors.

"What are you going to do if you are in an alley in 77th Division and a big, buffed out parolee?"

Beware of the big, black man. They never used that same scenario in relation to any other area of Los Angeles except in the southern portion of the city like the Southwest Division, Southeast Division, and Wilshire Division, the portions of the city concentrated with black people. What they did was like the military—conditioned the mind of the trainee. One condition was to fear the black man. If a recruit was already fearful and lacked understanding, respect, and compassion for all people, some of the training pushed the weak-minded into a dangerous mindset that all black people were criminals. That would play itself out in this and other incidents during police and community interactions.

The jokes seemed to come out of nowhere, but understood it was to let the black officers know black was inferior to white.

"What's black and brown and looks good on a black man? A Doberman."

"What's long and hard on a black kid? Sixth grade."

"How do you keep ten black guys from fighting? Throw them a basketball."

"How do black people teach their children to walk? They use chickens."

They did not intend for these jokes to be funny; it was stereotyping the black community.

I graduated with fifty-two of my classmates in January 1982. My assignment was to the 77th Street Division, described by LAPD's training staff as the roughest and most violent division in the city of Los Angeles. They claimed the community hated the police and nothing but "assholes" lived in 77th Street Division. It scared me to death. But wait, some of my best friends and family members lived in 77th Street Division, so not everybody could be bad.

From the first day in the Academy, to the last day of my probationary period, illustration of hatred toward the police was drilled into my head.

"Some soul brother gonna take your gun and kill you with it."

"What are you gonna do if a six-foot-five-inch, buffed out black parolee..."

"You're chasing a car full of Eight Trey gang members."

"A big, fat, black woman with a knife..."

Damn, does anyone else commit crimes other than black people?

ooooo

The mean streets of 77th Street Division in 1982, a few years after the Eula Love shooting by LAPD officers, was still on the minds of older officers and the community.

My first P-3 training officers were two white guys. One was a savvy veteran of about sixteen years and had just left a specialized unit against his wishes and the other was a young, brand new training officer who had the same interest in baseball I once had.

Excitement and fear filled my first day as a police officer. The young training officer explained as much as he could.

"What you learned in the academy, forget it. This is the real thing. The main thing is that you and I get to go home at the end of our shift. Got it?"

"Yep!" I replied.

"We treat people fair and respect everyone, but we don't back down from anyone."

"Okay!"

"We take bad guys to jail and we can help the old lady across the street."

I was thinking, *I am feeling good!*

"I have your back, you better have mine," he said.

I like this guy!

"Let's go get something to eat," he said and then radioed in. "12 Adam 15 requesting code 7."

"Okay, code 7," said the dispatcher

Shit, I forgot my wallet!

We get to a place to eat that is operated by and filled with black people. I felt funny seeing that everyone in the 77th

Division supposedly hated the police. At least, that was what the Academy's instructors tried to get us to believe.

"Hey, officers." The man appeared to own or manage the joint. "How are you? Have a seat."

"Sir, I don't have any money on me."

My training officer replied, "It's covered, don't worry."

We ate and the food was prepared, served, and graciously accepted for free.

"And everyone hates us here?"

After we ate, we drove around, we responded to assist other officers and I stood as if I was doing something. But, I had no clue what to do but follow and shadow my training officer.

As we continued to patrol, we got stares and the evil eye from roughnecks standing on the corners, two people took off and ran from us for reasons unknown to me, the rookie. We drove in residential areas and several people, mostly older, mature people waved hello, kids waved and said, "Police." I waved back and thought, *Something is not adding up.*

"Never ignore kids," said the training officer. "First impressions with kids and other people dictate our future relationships."

Deep, I thought, and nodded in agreement.

"Office needs help! Officer needs help! Shots fired! Shots fired 84th and Broadway!" The radio erupted in chaos. Officers talking over one another, the radio telephone operator, realizing an officer was in serious trouble, voice shrieked with helpless instructions to get others to the location to assist the officer in need.

This by far, was the worst call to hear. A brother officer screaming for help, and this was a motor officer (motorcycle) who often rides alone.

My mild mannered training officer screamed at me to put my seatbelt on and "Break out the tube."

Huh?

Get the shotgun out, now!"

As the radio filled with people screaming:

"Show me en route!

"Show me responding!"

What's the location?"

The radiotelephone operator screamed instructions to voices over the two-way communication, as voices trampled over one another. It was pandemonium.

My training officer was driving the "Adam 12" Plymouth Fury at break neck speed on residential streets, hitting dips, sparks flying from underneath, the engine roaring like a caged animal, the smell of burnt rubber and worn brakes filled the old worn interior of this symbol of the most popular police department in the world. As I held onto a loaded 12-gage shotgun pointed at the roof of the car, sliding across the vinyl bench seat and two red lights beam the warning—*here come the police*—and the backward facing ambers signaling—*there goes the police*—we arrive at the help call.

To my amazement, it looked like every single police officer on the force was at the location with more coming; helicopters, motorcycle officers, detectives. Shit, there were people with beards and scruffy clothes jumping out of beat up cars and vans with guns. It scared me to death. I sighed when I realized they were undercover officers. How was I to know? This was my first day on the J.O.B. *Wow!*

The downed officer was attacked with a knife, along with a stabbing victim. The officer shot the suspect. My job at the scene was to the keep the crime scene log. *Simple*, I thought, *I've got this; just take down names and serial numbers of EVERYONE who comes to the scene.*

"Brox, no one comes into the scene until they check in and out with you. You got it?" That came from my training officer.

"Yes, sir!"

Well, that did not work too well. There were some experienced and senior people showing up, including chiefs and the media. Some complied and gave me the information I asked for, but others barked, "Get the fuck away from me, boot." Boot is a term for a rookie officer. A fellow officer told me his name was Frank N. Stein and I wrote it down. Dumb me.

"May I have your name and serial number, please, for the log?"

A well-dressed manicured suit and tie VIP-looking man approached saying, "Do you know who this is?"

"But, was told—"

"Son, get out of the way," said the VIP.

I was failing badly.

In the sea of blue uniforms, flashing amber lights, similar looking people and cars, I felt like a lost child at a Fourth of July celebration at a county fair and I was looking for my mommy. By now, I could not locate my training officer and I was sure I would get fired because that log had about eight names on it and there were hundreds of people there.

It was 2300 hours (11:00 p.m.) and we were still at the scene. Our shift ended at 3:30 p.m. Tired and frustrated, we were on our way back to the station, and I had to come back here at 6:00 a.m.? I didn't know about that. There came that quitter mentality. At home, I called and woke up my mother to tell her about the day and my frustrations.

"Mom, I don't know if this is for me."

She prayed for me and told me, "God will never leave you nor forsake you. Take your bee-hine to work in the morning."

"I love you, good night."

I did just that, morning after morning, learning from this young, new training officer. He was a teacher, a patient and understanding man with a wife and young family. One of his sons had the same first name as mine.

"Hey, sir, thank you for naming your son after me," I joked.

He would shake his head and say, "Yeah, right!"

Actual training included traffic stops, issuing traffic tickets, and report writing. I hated that he bought other units' report type calls to get me used to talking to people and conducting preliminary investigations. But, I learned and I learned fast.

Tactical stuff like approaching in-progress robbery locations, what-if tactics, street survival procedures, and things seemingly boring, but critical to my safety and the safety of the community. Building searches seemed to be his favorite. He would find a business owner who had empty buildings. He had a relationship enough they would allow him to use their location to work on his tactics. So, he and I would practice, honing our skills, working as a team and on non-verbal communications—continuous eye contact, head nods, and that sort of stuff.

One day, in broad daylight, we stopped at a building and he suggested we work on building clearance. We get in this building and head downstairs. It was so dark; I could not see my hand in front of my own eyes. Then, he disappeared. I remembered, no talking. No verbal communications with your partner. But, I could not see him. I walked in the darkness, hoping my eyes would soon adjust enough to see my training officer, let alone a burglar., I felt someone was behind me. You know, that eerie feeling that someone or something is about to pounce? I turned around and he had his flashlight under his chin, illuminating only his face. It scared the shit out of me. He looked like Bela Lugosi in *Dracula*, but I played it off.

He went off on me. "Where is your flashlight?"

I had no answer. He scolded me about having *all* equipment with me at *all* times. I never forgot that.

He was a great example of what a community police officer should be; he was in touch with the people he served. He was hard on crime, but fair. He tried to shield me to some of the ugliness within the LAPD's 77th Street Division.

On one of our last days working together, a call of a "burglary suspect, there now," and this was his type of call. We backed up other units headed that way and were already at the scene. He had this look on his face I will never forget. His facial expression changed when the radio broadcast came out as to "who" was already at the scene and asked for the ETA (estimated time of arrival) of another specific unit. Yet, we continued to respond.

Upon our arrival, there were several "old school" officers at the scene, surrounding a large tree in front of a multi-unit apartment complex. As he and I exited our vehicle, I heard orders from the officer to "Come down now! Come out of the tree!" I looked up and there was a young, black man/kid perched in the tree hanging on. It looked like he was holding onto his mother's pant legs, scared and tired.

My training officer said, "Brox, get in the car. Let's go."

Confused, I asked, "Can we assist?"

"They don't need our help. Let's go."

"Okay!"

As we were leaving and making a U-turn, the young man / kid jumped or fell out of the tree. I saw straight sticks raining down on him, officers kicking him. *Oh shit, damn,* I thought.

"You do not want to be involved in stuff like that or you will end up fired or in jail," he told me.

We left and never spoke about that call again.

My next training officer was the savvy veteran, forced out from a specialized unit. He was white, tall, tan and a cabinetmaker by trade. He owned his own shop in the westernmost portion of 77th Street Division. He was very quiet, yet went about his business with professionalism. His method of training differed from the youngster. He trained by doing and handling many radio calls others avoided. Most LAPD field officers hated traffic collision investigation. They would actually see a horrific traffic accident and make a U-turn to avoid the investigation, never thinking someone may need their assistance. I digress.

He taught me to embrace *all* calls for service and not to fear learning something new or foreign. Hell, everything was new so let's get it. I did not know what I was asking for.

His favorite call was child abuse investigation. He had a soft spot for children. He was 77 Division's kid's knight in shining armor. Case in point, we were about to leave for the day when a call for service kept going unassigned.

"Buy that call," he told me. Man, I had met this girl. I was to meet her after work, and well, you know.

We arrived at the scene. The neighbor who called for service met us and told us she saw this woman was giving a merciless whipping to a naked little girl with a tree branch on the porch. We knocked on the door and a very large woman answered it. She was wearing a tank top and cutoff jeans and sweating profusely. She seemed to be out of breath. My training officer, in his calm demeanor, asked if we could come into her home. She allowed us in. The house was well kept, and pleasant. We told her why we were there.

"My neighbors called you guys," she said. She told us she was giving her foster child a whipping for lying. I heard the child whimpering in another room. We told her we were there for the safety and well-being of the child. She told us she used a switch from the tree, which was not too alarming as I, too, was whipped with switches. She showed it to us and said, "It was much bigger before the whipping."

"Can we see the child?"

She left us where we stood and returned with a little four- to five-year-old with welts on her arms, face, back, legs, and buttocks. The little girl was still naked and a few of the wounds were open and bleeding. I was shocked. My training officer placed handcuffs on the lady, picked up the switch, and told me to call for an ambulance. My heart broken as I dialed zero for the operator and told her we needed an ambulance for a victim of child abuse.

We spent eight hours in overtime caring for this tiny little one and processing the abuser. We finished booking the suspect at Sybil Brand Institute and, so fatigued and drained, we drove all the way back to 77 Division from the 10 Freeway near California State College Los Angeles with our guns still locked in the trunk. God looks after and takes care of those that tend his flock and little defenseless angels. Thank you, Jesus, for watching over my training officer and me.

When my training officer left the department with a winning settlement in his lawsuit for unfair labor practices and retaliation, I met up with him. He made cabinets for my house and I referred him to others. Miss you, man!

CHAPTER THREE

The Thunder Chicken

Look up the word thunder chicken and coward in the dictionary and you will most likely see a photo or image that resembles my next so-called training officer. I later found out how much racism he had in his heart when it slipped out one day. I will get to that story; this won't take long.

This guy lived through pleasing the "old schoolers." He was not an officer with seniority under his belt. He wanted to be one of the guys so badly; he did things like sitting on the back row, smoking cigarettes with his feet up on the table. His tie unclipped and the sleeves of his uniform rolled up to his forearms. When his name was called for roll, he would answer with a "Yo" or "Yes, Mother," in hopes to win favor from the real veterans. He did other things like throwing stuff at the young probationary officers who sat on the front row of roll call briefings. If anyone was an "ass," he was.

I recall he and I followed a car full of, what we believed to be, criminals into an alley. Once they stopped, only two guys were in the car. He, my tough training officer, was nervous and fidgety, as he always was when we had to put in real work. Once I searched both guys and handcuffed them, he told me to clear the car.

"Guns, partner!" I yelled, alerting him.

He panicked and pointed his gun at the handcuffed detainees. "I got 'em, Brox, call for a backup, and a supervisor."

I got on the radio and did what my training officer told me to do. The first unit to arrive to assist us was two veterans. Once they saw what we had and the situation was basic, they lit into me.

"What the hell are you calling a supervisor for, are you scared?"

I looked at my more experienced training officer who did not defend me and left me out to dry. He got on the radio, told the radiotelephone operator to cancel the supervisor request, and we have a code 4 and there was no need for an additional unit. He was a scary bastard!

His normal routine at the start our nighttime shift was to meet the vets at Florence and 8th Avenues for donuts at Winchell's Donut House. This one evening, he told me not to get out the car and gave me some old bullshit excuse. As I was sitting there, it was dusk, and I had the red light on inside to start my log. Something flew through the opened window and covered me, and my log, with a cold red liquid. I thought I was under attack. It was from my training officer.

"If I catch you asleep in my car I will kick your ass, Brox."

That jackass threw an extra-large fruit punch drink on me to get a laugh from the vets who sat there watching and laughing at me drenched with fruit punch.

"You are going to clean this car up before we leave here," he said.

"No, I am not," I replied.

The vets looked on and I heard, "Ooooh."

I asked him to take me to the station to change and he said "No" until one veteran said, "Take the kid back to the station, and forget about it."

So, he did, just like his "daddy" told him to do.

As we pulled into the station, he said, "If you tell anybody, I will tell the watch commander you were asleep in the car; I did it to wake you up."

I told the watch commander what happened. My training officer lied. I was reassigned with another training officer. That had a residual effect. When it was time to go eat, they would drop me off at the station and go eat with the vets and pick me up after their dinner. Mind you, I was the only black field officer on this shift.

The person I talked to was an old crusty Sergeant II, with Navy tattoos on his forearms, thirty-plus years of service, often wreaked of alcohol, and known to sip while on duty. He was a good guy to tell me to hang in there, ignore the jackasses, and learn the job.

The other black officer worked the uniformed desk, a senior desk officer who had been there for years, a veteran on the PD and an avid chain smoker. I often talked to him and his stories of racism in this agency were eye opening. He told me to hang in there because "They don't want you here, they want you to quit." He told me, "A young group of upstart black officers have to stick together and one day run this police department. The only way is to get past these idiots at this level, study, and become their bosses."

I found that unity among LAPD black officers was not what everyone thought. Hold on, much more on that later.

Here is a snippet; I had three black training officers. A fourth was not my training officer directly, but you will see the connection to all this BS shortly. These two black training officers were veterans; just out of vice unit and a specialized assignment, very popular 77th Division fixtures. Very nice guys; I have much respect for them, but they were not the most productive street cops at 77th Division. One was a three plus one, senior lead officer; the others were P3 training officers. Most of the time spent with them was nearing the end of my probation and I had most things at this level down packed. While out with these guys, felony arrests and tickets were few and far between. They spent most of their time servicing the female community, if you get my drift.

The fourth black training officer I mentioned was most likely the most feared and respected field officer at 77th Division. I still speak to him as I near retirement. He was a veteran Thunder Chicken and others tried to impress. One day, as I was off duty, driving on Manchester Boulevard, approaching Vermont with a lady friend in my passenger seat, a van pulled up next to me with the barrel of a gun pointed at me. I had frozen before I realized whose van it was. I relaxed and he sped off, laughing. I drove a very recognizable car with personalized license plates, which was why he pulled the stunt on me. Crazy! Black officers supporting each other!

With my days numbered at 77th Street Division, I was chosen to play on its softball team. We made it to the City Championship where we faced the Hollywood Division at a park in the Hollywood area. It was an evening game well attended as some of the best softball players in the department represented both teams. I was playing second base with the score: Hollywood–8 and 77th–7. I fielded a ground ball to end the inning and our last chance to tie the game was upon us.

Our pitcher was old with bad knees. He was third at bat, able to get a hit, but we needed a pinch runner. Guess who? Thunder Chicken! He should have never been on the team, but he was drinking buddies with some of the older guys. This clown was not good, but he could run. He never played much, so he did not know the rules.

One of our guys reached first on a walk. Now, we have the go ahead run on first with two outs, one of our best hitters is at the plate, and I am on deck. Thunder Chicken takes off and steals third base slides in the dirt and shit was flying into the air. He thought he had done something well. You cannot steal on slow pitch softball!

When the dust settled, the base umpire raised his fist, called old Thunder Chicken out—game over, we lost. Thunder Chicken was the laughing stock of both teams. Embarrassed, he tried to protest.

I walked over to him, put my hand on his shoulder, and said, "It's okay."

"Get your fucking hands off me, nigger. Brox, I will fucking deck you right here."

I'd had enough, so I let a one-two fly and down he went. He grabbed my legs and tackled me as I was still dropping those rights on his side and back. Several guys pulled us apart.

That punk-ass police officer tried to make a complaint, saying I punched him for making a mistake on the ball field. Both captains were there and witnessed the brawl. My captain was black and he later asked me if Thunder Chicken deserved getting hit and if I would do it again.

"If he called me out of my name again, I would do the same thing," I said.

"From what I heard, he had it coming."

As days went on, sitting in front of the roll call room, waiting for roll call and our assignments, some of the veterans who sat near the back of the room tossed a blazing dictionary toward me, almost hitting me. Yes, a flaming dictionary! And, probationary officers had to sit together on the front row. I turned around to see where that bomb came from.

A few guys yelled, "What the fuck you looking at, boot, turn around and face forward."

CHAPTER FOUR

Things I Will Never Forget About the 77th Street Division

The day a crazed man with a shotgun and a sword shot three of our officers at 76th and Figueroa, most of us ran to the scene from the station because we were in roll call. My close family friend and officer was shot in the face. I had dated his sister and their mother was my mother's next-door neighbor. The supervisor took me with them to this officer's mother's house because the news flashed that three 77th Street Division officers were shot. Once our caravan of police and detective vehicles arrived on my mother's street, people on the entire street were comforting my mother and this officer's mother. Everyone knew two Gardena men from this street worked at the 77th Street Division, but no one knew who it was. Imagine being a mother and not knowing if your son was shot, if he was dead or alive. As the entire residential street comforted each other, here comes a caravan of police vehicles onto your street.

My mother saw me get out of the lead vehicle and cried, praying, and thanking God for His blessings. But, the more difficult task was to tell my neighbor, the injured officer's mother, and his sister that her son, her brother, and my friend, my LAPD brother, had been shot in the face.

The tears, the emotions, the fears. Trembling and shaking, their mother grabbed me.

"Is my son dead? Is he dead?"

"No," I told her, "but we have to go now to the hospital." I told her he was strong and to pray.

My former girlfriend was holding my hand so tight it went numb. Her brothers were hurt. To the white officers and supervisors, it appeared their display was of anger. The way we (black folks) express pain and hopelessness makes white officers nervous. When I noticed the officers' demeanor, I assured them the brothers meant no danger.

My mother and the entire family of the down officer went to the hospital to support their son, brother, father, and husband. Officers from all over were also at the hospital. He lost an eye, but was very lucky and blessed, as the suspect was shooting No. 7 shot, not .00 Buck, or else it would have been very different!

ooooo

I was injured during an altercation with a PCP suspect. He had attacked his elderly mother and she called the police. Upon our arrival, my partner, an older black P-3, and I saw him standing on the porch railing kicking at the security bars. He was naked. We split his attention and as luck would have it, he jumped off the porch and started toward my old ass partner. I quickly approached the suspect from the rear and hit him with everything I had, a full baseball swing right across his back. He turned toward me with a look like *motherfucker*, and grabbed my baton. I was not going win that Tug of War with that guy, not while he was on that juice, so I resorted to what I knew best—street fighting. I grabbed him around his underarm and neck and twisted him down to the ground, trying to hold onto him to keep him away from the gun on my hip. I was losing my grip due to his sweat and Jheri Curl that was flopping all over the place. I could not let go. If I had, he would have been loose and free to pounce on me, my partner, and the old woman screaming, "Don't hurt my son!" She should have been screaming for us to kick his ass. My partner ran back to the car to call for help. He returned with his straight stick, and swung as if he was in a Kung Fu movie. He hit me more than he hit the suspect. I was getting the whooping of my life by my training officer, but I held on and never let that guy go. The troops arrived and subdued the suspect. Exhausted and unable to feel my hand, somebody called an ambulance. I only remember arriving to the hospital and doctors telling me I had a fractured elbow and a head contusion. Thanks, partner!

The last of many 77th Street Division stories; there are hundreds, but this one stuck with me. I responded to an ambulance shooting call one evening. The radiotelephone operator broadcasted that the suspect was still at the scene and still armed. Once I got there, I saw what appeared to be a male victim on the front lawn, bleeding profusely from upper body wounds. I waited for the other units to arrive and as they did, one officer had been to the location on several other occasions. He knew the players and the entire family history. Okay, so what was the plan?

He called out over the PA system. "Mrs. James, this is officer XXXX. Is it okay if we come in?"

"Hey, man, are you sure it's safe?"

He trusted Mrs. James and approached the kicked-in door. He came out, yelling, "Code 4," and, along with the ambulance crew, we approached the victim.

Nope, Mrs. James was an eighty-plus-year-old, partially blind lifelong resident of the house.

It turned out that the suspect/victim was her whacked out, PCP-using grandson who had kicked in her front door making threats and she opened fire with a rusty-as-hell, long barrel .22 8-shot revolver that looked like something out of a Dick Tracy cartoon. She emptied the eight rounds, hitting him in the upper body seven out of eight shots. Better percentage than any LAPD officer involved shooting!

My time at 77th Street Division was short in terms of a career. Those who said all the people in the area hated us were dead wrong. Hard working people who worked to support their families the best they could live in the area. Yes, some criminals just hated the police, but the number is few compared to the entire population of the division. Think about this, if *everyone* in the 77th Street Division hated the police and wanted us dead, which would be so easy to do.

Just before leaving the 77th Street Division, I was on loan to the Southwest Division. I was still new, but officially a P-2 dog, eager to hunt for bad guys. Along with several units, I responded to a call for service—man with a gun—at a bar near the Los Angeles Coliseum. He made threats to shoot everyone in the bar. Upon arrival, we were told he left the location. I took the report and we cleared the scene. Not too long after leaving, there was another call for service; man with a gun had returned to the location, this time a shot had been fired. We responded to the rear this time, as he escaped through the rear the last time. We were deployed behind dumpsters, police cars, and a block wall. We got an update that he was still inside the location. I was the closest to the rear door; he could not see me, but I saw him as he backed out of the bar's rear door, holding something in his hand as he screamed and cursed at the patrons of the bar. Still backing away, he turned. *Lord, am I going to have to shoot this man?* I thought. As he turned his right shoulder, he was holding a small black gun. As soon as he saw the police cars, he was startled, dropped the gun, and raised his hands. He followed instruction and we took him into custody. Code 4. He was a drunk. The shot fired was an accidental discharge.

A white senior officer approached me and said, "Brox, you just blew a great opportunity to shoot someone. It does not get any easier than that."

I was not there to shoot anyone, nor have I ever wanted to shoot anyone unless I had no other options, choice or a last resort!

ooooo

"Operator 347, may I help you?"

I thought to myself, *I am trained and ready.* A 77th Street Division-trained field officer, a P-2 dog ready to handle any field situation. Put me in a black and white as a two-man car or an L unit, and I will get the job done. I will serve with all my knowledge and keep the felons running and jails full.

The department sent my black ass to the Communications Division. "A real police officer answering phones; this is not what I was trained to do nor did I sign up for this," I said aloud. Despite my immature whining, I was now operator number 347. How degrading. I shook my head in disbelief. To top it off, my supervisors were not police officers. They were radiotelephone operator civilians. This shit kept getting better and better during that eight-hour communications training day.

Yet, I was there. One year they told me, only one year. While several classmates and other young officers were patrolling and chasing bad guys, I was in the company of a bunch of women operators. Carry a gun for what? I was in that room with a telephone sticking out of my ear and the only chase was a red light. If the red light was on then people were on hold. Hey, I serve and I am a member of the community. I would not want to call the police for someone to put me on hold, so I answered the phone.

As days went by, I embraced this new assignment. I chose to be me, so I spoke to people and met others. One day, at the start of my shift, I was socializing with some ladies and a radiotelephone operator supervisor, a rough-looking chick—a cross between Jimmy Durante and Ruth Buzzi—walked up to my side. With the lead point of a sharpened pencil, she poked me three times.

"I need you to plug in," she said.

I gave her a look as if to say, *Lady, poke me one more time, I will knock the crap out of you.* I guess it scared her.

Later that day, the watch commander called me into his office. The balding police lieutenant sat high above me and seemed to speak down to me about my attitude.

"We all have to be here. I know this is not your choice." *Damn right!* "But, I cannot have you trying to intimidate my staff. She is a supervisor and she demands your respect."

"Okay, boss, but please tell your supervisor not to poke me with a pencil."

"Brox, grow up. Get out of my office."

Later, I was in the break room and the lieutenant walked in. I thought he was on his knees, this short sawed off reject from the *Wizard of Oz*. Laughing aloud, he was the same height as that little dude that used to say "The plane, the plane" sitting in the big chair, raised to make himself seem bigger. I called him Tattoo, but only to myself, and others who also found humor regarding his stature.

I guess I was not great at dispatching. I got into trouble for using the wrong emergency codes a few times, so they sent me to the report writing room. They called it IRO (Information and Report Office). Now this was more like it, *not!*

We worked in a small room about four floors underground. I guess that was where they put the idiots. Had to be because I met this giant police officer—six-five, three-hundred-plus pounds, black P-2 with a Jheri Curl. His skin was dark, jet black. Blacker than train smoke. He was built like an upside down bowling pin—big up top and skinny on the bottom. More like a whiskey barrel on stilts. He was a bully, but manageable. He told me I was too little to be a police officer. I was five-eight, one hundred fifty-five pounds, so he would prove that I was too little, dang near daily. Using his superior size (dang near the same size as a low land gorilla), he grabbed me (in uniform and in the workplace), threw me to the ground, and pinned me motionless in front of others. I took my ass kicking like a helpless little girl. He also bullied most of the other guys in IRO, like an overweight veteran, whom he called *slob*. He also called another veteran guy *filthy* and called me *shoebox* for the shape of my head. No issues, I could play the dozens with the best. I gave him back the business and called him a *giant raisin*. I told him to stop coming into the office naked. "Oh, I am sorry. You do have your uniform on." We had fun going back and forth. It made the nights go by faster. The place was the pits and I had to get out of there and soon.

But, not before I took advantage of the crops. Women overran that place. Hundreds. Some good looking, some not so good looking. Sworn officers were in short demand, and it appeared the pretty and ugly women were hunting for men, regardless of how we looked. I recall this brother, who was not that easy on the eyes, was a virtual sex machine to several different ladies at the Communications Division.

A well-known fact throughout the department was that the single women (married ones not excluded) of communications were on the prowl to land a husband (get that dual income and pension) or give up the goodies, get pregnant and get that child support. Or, used that moneymaker (pussy) to trap an officer. Some of the young sworn female officers were no different.

There were several incidents at parties and outings, and the communications floor. Altercations included women who were fucking the same police officer.

One incident in particular, a Southwest Division officer was hitting two or maybe even more communications women at the same time. Two black women found out about each other and they clashed. Fighting like cats, hair flying and nails breaking, screams of pain and anger, insults flying, shoes scattered, clothes torn, and tits exposed.

The fight occurred on the floor of the communication room, in front of everybody and they both dropped the air (they were radiotelephone operators in contact with field officers). That was entertainment. Oh, I forgot, those two combatants were squabbling over a married-with-children brother. Help *my* people, Lord.

It did not stop there. The guy they were fighting over got into a brawl with a fellow officer while in uniform over one of these chicks. It turned out that one of the cat fighters was the single guy's girlfriend or fiancé.

Getting pussy from the women at communications was easy as walking and breathing. If an officer was alive and walking upright, he could get laid, if he wanted.

I mentioned that I took advantage. Well, I did not. I did my dirt and slept around, but not at that place. I recall one sister there; fine as hell, but she was trouble. She asked me to come by her house after work. She lived in Downey, California.

No pre-dates, no getting to know each other, no warm up, or anything. I arrived at her apartment—very nice place, clean, beautifully decorated with African art and pleasant smelling. No dinner. No talk. She wanted to fuck. Err, nope! I was not falling for it.

"What's wrong?" she asked me.

I told her I had a girlfriend.

She stood in front of a gas fireplace. The sheer multicolored wraparound garment she wore showed her curvy body, full thick breasts, and flat stomach illuminated by the flames.

I gasped and she reached toward me. The garment slowly opened and displayed her golden flesh and the erect nipple of her breast. *Oh shit*, I said to myself. She was one of the fine ones. But, I stood firm (literally) and rebuffed her advances. No pussy that night for me. I stayed awhile. She acted as if it was okay.

"I understand," she said.

I thought it was all-good.

Forgot where I was working, a place full of cackling ass women who told everyone's business, including their own.

A couple guys, including the black incredible bulk asked me, "Michael, tell me the truth, you went over her house and did not fuck her?"

Embarrassed, I played it off as any twenty-two-year-old would. "I don't know what you are talking about."

This went on for a while. The next thing I knew, two ladies at Communications Division were asking me if I was a fag. Whoa, me? Not hardly.

Big man started in on me, saying, "Come here, you little faggot," all because this woman told her communications buddies I refused her sexual advances.

I had to get the fuck out of that place! Too sleazy, even for me! A year passed before my reassignment to a place where *all* brothers and sisters go—Wilshire Division.

CHAPTER FIVE

"The Plantation"

I arrived to Wilshire Division in late 1983. I could have kissed the ground there. I was happy to be away from the Peyton Place-type drama of communications and the overt racism of some officers in the 77th Street Division.

I noticed something odd. There were black officers everywhere at this division. Great, I now remember the word of the old wise veteran, chain-smoking brother at the 77th Street Division desks. Now, we (black brothers and sisters) can take care of each other.

"The Plantation" was a name allegedly given to the Wilshire Division due to the high number of black officers working "the field" there.

The economic and social dynamic of Wilshire as a patrol division was unsurpassed by any place in Los Angeles. Just before the southern end of the division, right across from the station was a community of apartments, and multi-unit dwellings; the neighborhood gangs referred to the area as the "School Yard." Most of the residents were black and Hispanic.

Two to three miles north was a more affluent area where black and whites lived together. And north of that was the Wilshire high-rent district, where celebrities and rich folks with old money lived: Muhammad Ali, Donna Summer, Lou Rawls, the Mayor's house, and countless others. The northeast was Korea Town, drive through there and it was difficult to find a billboard advertisement in English.

The east side was mostly Hispanics and the west was a mixture of hardworking families, very nice single-family residences with some apartments. And, the northwest—mostly north—was exclusive to mostly white folks or a large Jewish population.

So, it was a great place to work; exciting, challenging and it felt like a brotherhood. But, not all that glitters is LAPD gold.

I was a part of a three-person car, three former athletes (Snake, Speedy and Bullet and Stone). My nicknames were Speedy and Bullet. Now, at my advanced age, they call me Speed. We had a ball putting in work on the streets of Wilshire, making arrests, writing tickets, and chasing women (in our spare patrol time). The master of that department was Snake, need I say more. Stone was a weightlifting, bodybuilding, soft spoken, serious minded ex-football player who had supreme confidence and faith in his ability at anything, which often got him in hot water.

We worked a shift called the morning watch from 11:00 p.m. to 6:00 a.m., the graveyard shift. We rotated days off; when one was off, the others worked together. Normally in Wilshire, most of the Division would shut down around 1:00 or 2:00 a.m. The only things opened at those hours were Juicy Lucy's, a few coffee and donut shops, night clubs (The World Night Club, The Bitten Apple, and The Red Onion), so there was a lot of down time.

Stone was the master of catching a wink or two during our shift. He never wanted to be the driver; he always wanted to keep books. I took a while to figure it out, though. That is where the name "Stone" came from and I bet most people thought it was because of his physical appearance. Nope, it was because this brother could sit in the passenger seat of a moving police vehicle, look straight ahead, and not move a muscle. And, he had a lot of muscle. He wore sunglasses during darkness once we hit the streets, lights out. He was gone; sleep before we made it to the first traffic light. Stone would wake up if things called for him to act. He would normally come back to life around 5:00 a.m., when traffic was moving, and write a couple of tickets at a Wilshire cherry patch to justify his and our stats.

Don't believe the command staff and the hype, LAPD may not have a printed quota, but if you come in empty handed (tickets or arrests) you would find yourself assigned to the desk, the jail, or handing out equipment to more productive officers. You may handle *all* the radio calls for service; no tickets, no arrests, just sit your ass in the station, and look forward to a warm evaluation.

I quickly found out that promotions and specialized assignments were very competitive. So competitive that several black brother and sister officers would sell themselves out and drop another sister or brother to get that promotion. I was not ready for promotions as I was having fun with my partners and still single with no children. I played at lot of sports: football (where Speedy came about) softball, basketball (I was terrible at basketball, just fast), and the Police Olympics (track and field, softball and my final appearance was flag football). I saw people (brothers mostly) stepping all over each to get special assignments.

Yet, when they got those jobs (vice, narcotics, senior lead), they would never reach back and pull another brother along. I recall one brother who worked the graveyard shift with us. He was a P3, more senior to most of us. He was a good dude, but the biggest ass kisser I have ever seen. I was embarrassed for him. He was like that snitch or the teacher's pet, continually in the face of the watch commander, our lieutenant. A native of Hawaii named him Abdul Suck Butt. We all laughed, but it was truly pitiful. This brother had an agenda and no one would keep him from his goal. Heck, there's nothing wrong with that, but give some advice to others in order to get to where there was a need for more of us black officers. I guess his thought was, *Naw, boss, I ain't gonna let no other coloreds in here, no sir.* Others had to file lawsuits in order to reach his position and perhaps only if he spoke up for those who were truly qualified, the city would have to pay monies and force those into positions they did not want or that no one stood up for.

I worked hard at Wilshire and I played hard, too. I had the arrests and stats to match anyone at the division; I worked the Special Problems Unit (SPU) and often led my patrol watch in felony arrests, warrant arrests and tickets.

ooooo

It was 1984 and The Olympics was in Los Angeles. I, like others, worked the games for cash by working during my vacation. I was on a special detail at UCLA and on the field at the Coliseum. It was a great experience. I got married in October 1984 to my one and only wife and people from near and far came to bid us well wishes. It was a great day.

I matured fast. I needed to make more money because this new wife of mine was demanding and money was an issue. I promised her to take care of us, but I was terrible with finances. So, I figured I needed to promote. P3 opportunities came along, so I put in for two positions. I reached out to black officers (in those special assignments) and black supervision at Wilshire. Few gave me the time of day. I recall one brother, who was an established P3, told me, "Brother, if I help you, I have to help everybody. I did this on my own." I was no threat to him or anyone else; there were enough positions to go around. Being educated, a hard worker, and experience and stats to back it up, I went out "on my own" and landed flat on my back. I was not even considered in the running, even though there were two positions and five applicants—me, a brother from another division, and three white girls: two from Wilshire and one from outside. Both white girls were selected.

I reached out to a sergeant (a brother) who was on the board and he told me I had to learn to "play the game." I was still wet behind the ears and sought the guidance of some of the black detectives in Wilshire. A senior detective, whom I will always respect, gave it to me straight. He said, "You have to be twice as good as white officers," and that was helpful. He told me that stats alone were not good enough. Rumor was that no one took me serious. He told me to stop all the jokes, "shucking and jiving," and mature quickly. He said as an example, he heard that during a uniform inspection, I had my shoes on the wrong feet. He laughed. I had to admit it and I chuckled, too. He said, "They don't forget that kind of stuff." That was eye opening.

I started being more business minded; more reserved and took leadership roles at crime scenes and in the station. A white sergeant pulled me aside and asked me if I was okay. "Mike, you just don't seem to be your normal self." That shook me; I was trying and all this white supervisor saw in me was buffoonery. Change was coming.

I kept at it and I received a P3 position after two more interviews. More money, more money. Wife was still not financially satisfied. Dang it. I trained new officers right out of the Academy. I knew I needed to make a positive impression on them and help keep them to stay alive for our LAPD family and their own. So, I took pages out of my first two training officer's books. We worked on tactics, building searches, made sure their equipment was in working order and they knew how and when to use it per department guidelines. It was an honor to be trusted to train our new officers. I was on my way to being a respected senior officer.

I had the pleasure of training officers that later became chiefs of police at other agencies, captains, detective supervisors, lieutenants, law professionals and heads of departments teaching at prestigious universities. Most are at retirement age now. I am proud to say I may have had just a small influence on their professional development.

Not all of them had it that easy. One case I had to fight for was that of an older Korean probationer. He came to the United States from Korea after serving in their military for several years. LAPD hired him and he graduated from our academy. He was sent to Wilshire for his probationary evaluation and training.

Before me, he had other training officers, including "Abdul Suck Butt," who treated this guy with such racially motivated bias that it was impossible for him to learn. This guy was not a child, not a twenty-one-year-old thunder cat. He served in the military, raised a family and was here to learn. He had a heavy Korean accent when he spoke. Often, when he would speak over the radio, several white and some black officers would make shitty comments, making light of his tongue. How unprofessional and disheartening for him, trying to learn and to hear "wha' happin'" after his broadcast. I'd had enough of it. They told me he was going to be terminated because of his unsatisfactory evaluations. I asked the supervisors to allow me, a senior P3, to take him on and give him another shot at this job. He was no better or no worse than any other probationer at his level and time in training. The only thing that stood out was he was sometimes difficult to understand in situations of stress such as following a stolen car where an officer had to quickly call out street names and the description of the speeding vehicle attempting to elude capture.

He showed me he belonged on this job and I evaluated him as such. However, they proceeded with termination proceedings. As it would be, his representatives saw my satisfactory evaluation that contradicted those of the biased and unfair officers. So, they called upon me to speak on his behalf. I did just that. Later on at the station, some of the white officers and supervisors made comments that I was going to be held responsible if someone working with him got killed because he did not know what to do. Yeah right. He is still on this job, a detective supervisor in a specialized unit.

Regardless of race or gender, not every person is cut out for police work. One such case was that of a very introverted young black officer. He was assigned to be trained by a very experienced, Metro-trained brother.

The young probationary officer made mistake after mistake. His training officer tried and tried to help him pass probation. One night, on a hot call of a shooting in progress, the young officer and his training officer were on the call for several hours. They got back into the patrol car to head back into patrol mode.

"Hey, did you step in some dog shit?" the training officer asked his probationer.

They got out of the car to check their boots. Officers often get doo-doo lodged in the grooves of their combat boots. They had no visible evidence of crap on their shoes. They got back in the car and headed on their way; the smell increased and was almost unbearable. The training officer looked over at his probationer. A tear was rolling down the side of the young man's face.

"Are you crying? What's wrong?"

The probationer asked if they could go to the station to change. "I had an accident."

The training officer looked at him, stunned. "Did you boo-boo on yourself?"

The probationer confirmed that he had shit his pants.

Police officers are brutal. The news spread like loose bowels. Other officers lit into the young officer with jokes and nicknames. The one that stuck was "Boo-Boo." From that point, the young officer could do nothing right and shortly thereafter he made some very critical and unsafe mistakes. He realized he was not cut out for a career in law enforcement and no longer wanted to be a police officer. He resigned.

Racism and bias still rears its ugly head, even in the '80s. I was working the field and "Officer requesting a backup, Crenshaw and Washington," came across the radio. The request was actually considered really urgent. It came from a K-9 officer and normally these macho guys could handle anything. My young partner and I raced through traffic, blowing red lights even if we were not authorized to respond with light and sirens. The K-9 officer sounded like he needed more than a backup as his voice elevated and had terror and urgency all in it. We cut across a gas station; almost hit a pedestrian and dang near collided with a red Volkswagen and finally arrived at the scene. We blocked traffic with our vehicle, got out and ran to the east side of the street. This K-9 officer was holding onto this brother, about six-foot-three and two hundred twenty-five pounds, who was already handcuffed, screaming, "My daughter is in the car, man, my daughter is in the car! Get my daughter!" The K-9 officer was also trying to keep his dog from biting this guy. So up came this skinny milk toast white officer who was known as a cage rattler at Wilshire. He was the first to reach the black guy. This officer grabbed him in a c-clamp (hand around a person's front portion of the neck, cutting off the airway). My female partner (RIP) heard the man screaming for his child. She got the child out of the car.

I was trying to help calm the man down, so I tell milk toast, "Let him go, I got it, let him go!"

He did and gave me a look as if to say, *What's your problem, buddy?*

The man was obviously drunk, but started to calm down when he saw his daughter in the hands of my partner. He said that was all he wanted, to get her out of the car. He kissed her (not my partner, his daughter) and we all went to the station to finish booking him for drunk driving and to get the little one to her mother.

While assisting the K-9 officer with processing, a white sergeant (the same one who asked if I was okay) asked me to meet him in the office.

"What's up, Sarge?"

"Hey, Mike, what is this I hear you coming between one of my officers and his arrestee?"

I explained that the guy simply wanted his daughter and he was very agitated, handcuffed and the other officer did not need to aggravate the man any further. I stepped in as the senior and was able to calm the man down.

"Mike, I need to know, whose side are you on?"

"I'm on the side to do the right thing at the right time. I'm not aware of an *us versus them*. I serve the public."

"Mike, make sure you don't alienate yourself from your brother officers."

I remember that to this day. In light of what is and always has been going on, that is the real problem—law enforcement cannot serve the public if law enforcement puts this barrier of US vs. THEM.

I was the second patrol unit at the location of one of the most famous murders during my time at Wilshire Division. I responded to an early morning shooting on Gramercy Place with a few other officers. We cleared the house and I saw the victim on the floor bleeding pretty bad. It did not look good for him at all. Family members were screaming and crying. It was a mad house. As I went down the stairs to make sure an ambulance was en route, I noticed all these awards and gold records on the walls and it hit me, "Somebody really likes music." I quickly verified the status that rescue was on the way and reentered the location. An officer who had an older man detained told me it was Marvin Gaye.

"Who? The victim?"

"Yep." The officer, a good friend, had a look on his face, like *this is gonna be big*. We called the detectives and the rest was Motown and music history.

On another case I will never forget, my partner was a deep, baritone-voiced brother whose voice was better suited for a radio disc jockey. He was a popular dancer in the early stages of locking, which is a style of funk dance. He danced his way onto *American Bandstand* in the 1970s with his own crew. He was known as Sinbad. Well, I guess that did not pay the bills, so now he was a LAPD Wilshire police officer. He is a very good friend.

We responded to an unknown trouble call in the well-to-do northern portion of town. This type of call is very dangerous. There was no additional information, no one to call back and give further details or a reporting person to meet. We arrived at a very well manicured apartment complex. The building's front door was ajar. That was somewhat strange, yet we pushed on. In the lobby, there were fresh droplets of blood near the elevator and an exit door about twelve feet to the west of the building.

We called for the elevator. The building had only three floors. My partner suggested we try the stairs for safety. We did and as we came to the first floor, we saw more blood on the door—number 114. We slowly walked toward the door. It was not closed and dark inside. We shined our stream light SL-20s into the interior, pushed the door with the butt of the flashlight to avoid leaving prints and contaminating the potential crime scene and entered the apartment. There was a lot of blood that covered a white couch and something protruding out the back of the couch. We announced our presence in a low tone voice, "Police department," then a bit louder, "Police department!" No one responded. The phone rang. *Oh, shit.* As we passed the front of the couch, there was a naked person (unable to distinguish the gender) cut to shreds. I had never seen anything like that; blood was everywhere, splattered on the walls, floors and this person was obviously dead, killed not too long before we arrived. The body was covered in slash and stab wounds. My partner located some evidence—a broken, bloodstained knife, the handle and blade were broken. Somebody was enraged. We stepped out into the hall and called for the detectives. No need to call an ambulance, this person's head was nearly severed off. As we waited just outside the door, we heard a faint voice.

""Hello. Hello, somebody."

"Did you hear that?"

A neighbor came out and said, "Is the old man okay? Is his son okay?"

An old man was inside the house during the murder. He was very old, could barely see or hear.

He asked, "Is my son okay?"

I won't go too much into detail about the injuries to the victim, but certain parts of his anatomy were missing, which made it difficult to tell if he was male or female. The person who made the call for service was the suspect, the victim's boyfriend. Other responding officers captured him on the bottom floor, injured and bleeding. He had never left the building. Turned out to be a crime of passion, Love hurts!

CHAPTER SIX

Dreams or Nightmares

I have been an avid dog person all my life. As a young boy, I would find dogs and have them follow me home. I would teach them to sit, stay and come to me without any formal training or instructions. As I got older, I wanted to raise my own dogs from puppies. I had German Shepherds and Pit Bulls. I would walk them without leashes and have them perform for friends.

I had this idea. Why not be a K-9 handler with the police department? My uncle and a neighbor were K-9 handlers in the military and we talked about dogs all the time. The right dog could be brave, intelligent and loyal.

In 1985 or 1986, five positions became available in LAPD's K-9 unit. I was excited at the chance to be a new K-9 handler. The only problem was that these positions were in Metropolitan Division. Metro Division consisted of a large majority of white officers. When applying for Metro, they ask for a Polaroid photo of each applicant. This photo is placed on a board in the locker room and if an applicant's photo is turned upside down, that applicant will never get selected intro Metro.

I was not discouraged by the lack of brothers in Metro, so I put in my paperwork. Not only did I put in my paperwork, I created a mapping system to present to the interview board showing my home and the distance to each division, citywide. Also, I made the maps of each local heliport to allow the departments to make tactical K-9 transportation. (K-9 officers are often picked up by department aircraft to get them to scenes quickly.)

I also built kennels and dog runs in my yard, emulating those the department uses for established K-9s housed at central station.

I studied K-9 search criteria, policy on bites and medical treatment and notification of dog bites. Basic tactics and advanced handling by speaking to former and current military K-9 handlers.

I was also a member of LARK, the Los Angeles Rottweiler Klub, a civilian dog training and competition group that promotes dog health, solid dog training and K-9 companionship. I was in the group with my two Rottweilers and I was able to get titles on both. I was the handler and trainer along with the entire group headed by some very influential people.

I titled my dogs in Tracking, Obedience and Protection. One of my dogs, personally trained by me and a group of trusted Klub members and friends, was judged in the above categories by a German Judge, flown in by the United States Rottweiler Club. My dog and I competed in Lake Elsinore, California, and received V-rated for conformation and 90s in Tracking, Obedience and Protection. I had plenty of police experience, well read on matters pertaining to K-9 operations and my experience with dogs was unmatched by the seven candidates that applied for five spots.

There was a pre-test to get to the interview for the K-9 position. It's called a Metro PFQ, a physical fitness test that consists of a mile-half run in the hills of Elysian Park, bar pull-ups, sit-ups, push-ups and a weight drag. I took this test, finished second on the run, did seventeen pull ups, maxed out the number of sit-ups in the allotted time and maxed out the push-ups. I was able to drag the weight the required distance without any problems. So, I passed.

I wanted this job really bad. I went beyond the posted job requirements. At the time, there was one black K-9 handler of ten. There were only seven applicants for five positions. I was pretty sure I could be one of the five. After the interview, I was notified that I was not selected for the position. "Of the six candidates, we selected five individuals who we feel will best serve as new members of the unit. Good luck in the future."

Wait a minute. I thought seven people took the interview. I later found out that the other guy was promoted to sergeant and passed on the interview. So everyone who applied was selected but me. I was crushed and embarrassed. I found out that no one had ever done the preparation I had done for this or other Metro interviews.

Over the years, I applied for Metro K-9 nine times—count 'em, nine times—only to be rejected every single time. The last interview for a K-9 position was for a K-9 trainer. I applied for it. Prior to the interviews, I was anonymously sent copies of the candidates' pre-interview evaluation sheets. All ten of the applicants were evaluated on several factors, including experience, knowledge, and other factors. I studied all the sheets, yet I was the only person NOT assigned to the K-9 unit. What I saw shocked me. My evaluation score was the third highest score of all the candidates.

I called an attorney. I wanted blood. All those interviews and to be rated that high for a training position and not be selected for not one of the fourteen previous K-9 positions angered me. I told the attorney everything that happened to me over the years as I tried to get one of these K-9 positions. He told me to take this final interview. I showed up and these two assholes—a bleached, white-haired white lieutenant and a balding sergeant (both served on my previous K-9 interviews) refused to give me an interview. I was speechless when the lieutenant asked, "Officer Brox, why are you back here again? There is nothing more to ask you in this interview." He looked at the balding sergeant who nodded in agreement. I stood there for what appeared to be minutes. He finally told me, "Good day, Officer Brox."

Later, I took my complaint to the bureau chief, a longtime member of the department, a black man who appeared to be well respected. However, he was a lame duck on his way to be a chief of another agency. He offered to just put me in Metro, but with a warning, "You know that is not going to be popular with them. They will do everything in their power to make you fail, but if that is what you want, I can put you there and you will be on your own." *What kind of shit is that*, I thought. Here is a bureau chief and he is acknowledging that members of OUR police department, predominately-white members of Metro, will intentionally sabotage another member's stay in an LAPD unit. This is absolute madness.

I went home to my wife and asked her. She was very aware of how bad I wanted to be a K-9 handler and all the stress I was going through to make it happen. She looked me in my eyes and asked me a simple question, while holding our newborn baby girl in her arms. "Baby, is it really worth all that?" For the sake of my family and my safety, I gave up my dream of being a K-9 handler. You kept me and others who look like me out and eventually ran out the ones that were there. LAPD Metro and the K-9 unit—FUCK YOU!

The last dig by members of the K-9 unit. My dog-training group and I were at the Academy after an evening of training. We were there with our dogs. Their dogs were in kennels, my dog was out, had just voided his bladder on some bushes and I placed him on a down stay. This K-9 officer pulled up and asked if we were police officers. I told him I was. He asked me if that was my dog on the grounds and told me I could not have my dog at the Academy. When I disagreed with him, he called his K-9 sergeant. The sergeant ordered me to place my dog in my truck and leave the property. I asked him why and he responded by saying, "Only police dogs are accepted on Academy grounds." I knew that was not true. I saw people with their dogs there all the time. We got into this discussion about dogfights and liability and I told him that I would put my dog away, but I was not leaving because this is MY Academy, too.

The next couple of days I was informed that I was the subject of a complaint by this Metro sergeant—insubordination the complaint read. I went through an investigation and the whole thing was dismissed.

One would wonder, how could a police department allow its members to be treated in such a manner? Its' very simple, I am black in blue and there is racism within the ranks of the LAPD.

Fast forward to 1986 or 1987. After being denied earning a position in Metro, I went back to patrol and for some reason I was making a statement that I was good enough to work any special assignment.

I started to work in the field to gain acceptance. Not acceptance by the people I was sworn to protect and serve, not because crime was running rampant, not because of anything else other than "I will show them."

I was becoming what I swore to myself, my mother and our Heavenly Father that I would never do. I was becoming a part of the US.

I was being rude to my community. I was less caring and less empathetic. I felt myself being more of an administrative kiss-ass to garner acceptance by those that shut me out.

My partner, Stone, saw something different in me. He called me on it and said, "Bullet, what is going on with you, man?" He watched me treat an elderly couple on a call for service with total lack of respect and downright rudeness.

He pulled me aside. "You are out here acting like some of these white boys," he said, which was something he had noticed over a few weeks. I heard him but I did not listen. My trusted partner, who I know would be there for me, was trying to get me back to Brox. I changed and others noticed as well.

My other partner, Snake, changed shifts and worked with someone else. I acted as if I did not care, told myself that I needed to do things for me and if no one understood that, too bad for them, I was going to be all right. I didn't need them anyway.

I was working with a white guy. He was okay, sort of a shit magnet. Every case he touched turned to shit in the blink of an eye. Early one Sunday morning, just south of Wilshire Boulevard and east of Western Avenue, as I drove the police car slowly through the neighborhood, I noticed a gray vehicle, doubled parked with its back passenger door open. As I got closer, I saw a small group of Asian women clutching their bags to their chest, huddled near each as they were backing away from a tall thin black man. He looked in our direction as we approached and quickly turned toward us, raised his hand and I saw a flash. Did this motherfucker just shoot at us!

He jumped into the rear seat of the gray car. My partner was screaming on the radio, "Officers need help, and shots fired 211 suspects." He gave our location and the car chase was on. Later, I found out he gave a location about one-half mile north of our actual location.

The suspect's vehicle was driving like someone left the gates of hell open. I was driving like a fool, too. The suspect's car flew through red lights and stop signs like it was the only one on the road. I floored it to keep up. My car was a piece of crap, with no get up and go. It started smoking and it appeared that we would lose him as the car screeched across Olympic Boulevard at about eighty miles per hour.

"Come on, Brox, floor it, they are getting away!" my partner screamed.

"Shut the fuck up!" I replied. His job was to broadcast our position at every turn so our assisting officers would be able to help us catch these "armed" robbery suspects. Funny, I did not hear him saying anything on the radio.

The driver of that "get-away" car was a maniac, but his ass overrode his skill, as he barreled down a slight hill at break neck speed. He tried to make a quick left onto a very small street with a dip in the roadway. "Oh, God! Oh my, God!" I screamed like a church girl. His car went airborne and now this three thousand pound flying car was headed right for a little boy standing next to a bicycle. The car narrowly missed the boy, crashed into the chain link fence of a corner house, and came to rest on its side in the residential yard. The little boy's mother, pushing a stroller, flew toward her son who was now on the ground. I thought the vehicle had hit him, but it did not. He was so scared; he dropped the bike and peed in his pants.

We stopped our car, red blue and yellow lights still flashing, breaks burning and smoke everywhere and sirens still blaring. The collision kicked up so much dust we could hardly see. But one of the robbery suspects, a shorter black guy somehow got out of the car and took off running southbound on the sidewalk.

"Partner, stop! Partner, no, come back!" Like a slew footed speeding camel, my partner took off after this obvious much faster younger and more athletic suspect that had a Ph.D. in running from the police. Where the hell was my back up? Where was the help? Oh, I forgot, my partner was not broadcasting. "Damn, by myself."

All of a sudden, this lanky brother was climbing out of the vehicle. I broke leather (pulled out my firearm) and ordered his crooked ass onto the ground.

"Naw man, I'm hurt, I did not do nothing." He kept walking toward me. He was much taller than me and got taller as he got closer.

"Get on the ground, man, now!" He kept coming, slowly but steady. I had no baton, no Taser or anything except what God gave me and what Stone and Snake helped me get in Wilshire's weight room. I put my gun away, walked toward this lanky punk motherfucker and let a right hand go. *BAM!* Right on the button. He stumbled backward and down he went. I put all my five-foot-ten, one hundred eighty pounds on his ass. I then quickly jumped on his back and handcuffed him.

Some onlooker neighbors, who had come out at the sounds of the collision and our sirens, jumped in to help me and the family that almost met with certain death.

All of a sudden, one of our responding officers was running to my position. "Ooo wee, ooo wee! I saw that shit. You knocked that motherfucker out. Where is your partner?"

Good question. I had no answer.

I swear to you, I never saw anything like this. This officer, my partner and ex-cop from New York who wears white socks with his uniform, never answering the radio was driving up to the scene in a blue minivan, parking light dangling as a result of a minor collision. The other suspect was in custody, seat belted in the front seat of this family van.

I could not believe what I was seeing. This goofy S.O.B. told us and the field sergeant that he was losing the suspect and could not catch him. He commandeered a van from an Asian lady and chased the suspect underneath the 10 Freeway until the suspect could not run any further. How do we write this up? *I am getting too old for this shit! Before I really screw up, I need a change personally and professionally.*

ooooo

Those in the department that have served more than thirty years often will say there is no racism within LAPD. That is bullshit!

Our own Chief Gates publicly said that genetically black people are "different" than "normal people." He was referring to numerous deaths by the use of the choke holds. He also made comments about hiring practices and his opinion that black officers were hired by means of political necessity and the standards were lowered to get us hired. "We will take them (blacks, women, and Hispanics) and err on the side of numbers." He said mistakes were made hiring blacks, women, and Hispanics, never once mentioning some of the white police officers who have been fired, arrested, and charged with crimes. So, I guess they (white officers) were not mistakes.

Detective Trainee

The department had a program called the Detective Trainee Program. It was a four-year commitment for those who had the desire and aptitude to work criminal cases. A trainee would be selected from a group of applicants to work in a geographic division alongside seasoned detectives. The trainee would learn case management, interview and interrogation techniques, the rules of evidence, court testimony as an expert witness, search warrant preparation and many more Law Enforcement related tasks.

I applied and I was accepted to be one of the trainees. One rule was that a trainee must pass the detectives examination and he/she must be promoted to the rank of detective within the four years or the trainee would be sent back to patrol. That would be embarrassing!

I started my first day in detectives, finally a special assignment. I was wearing my best suit and tie, flashy shoes, looked and smelled like a million bucks. My boss and his assistant were two older white super veterans. My boss had over thirty years of service and his assistant, an ex-Metro guy had dang near thirty years himself.

They looked at me, standing there on a Monday morning. "You are not going to a night club, don't wear that shit again. This

is no glamour or fashion show. Come tomorrow, you will see why."
I was assigned to the CAPS (Crimes Against Persons), which
were all crimes where someone, anyone "jumped on" someone
else. We handled fights, stabbings and shootings (if no one died)
disputes between neighbors, husband and wife and anything else.

I sat down and had no clue what I was to do, so the assistant
table coordinator, the ex-Metro guy, strong, tanned and slick
talking dropped about ten tan colored packages onto the desk
where I sat. They landed with a thud. "We had twenty-three
custodies over the weekend, welcome to CAPS." These were
people in jail and needed to be presented to the District Attorney
or City Attorney by eleven o'clock the following Tuesday morning.
What the heck have I gotten myself into?

I quickly got the hang of the custody thing. Just as I was
getting a handle on the speed and paper flow, I realized there
were reports that need addressing. Most of the reports were minor
fights and scraps but occasionally there was a need to get off the
chair and do something called an "investigation." Most of our
cases had to be turned in by ten days. I had over two hundred
cases alone a month, plus forty to forty-five custodies a month.
I was busy, but learned fast. My trainer taught me how to "cut
corners." We had the highest clearance rate and the less overdue
case in the history of Wilshire CAPS. They did an audit, we got
caught and we were split up. Unappreciative bastards!

I was starting to enjoy this detective thing. I had weekends
and holidays off and kind of on my own. This was okay. I was
assigned to the robbery table. The boss was an old school redneck.

He hated black folks and pretty much hated everybody. He was a sour old man with all white hair. The meanest old fart in detectives. He had several fallouts with some of the veteran black detectives. He would talk openly on how this person (black) was "a lazy piece of shit" and how that person (black) would never work his table.

They sent me to his table. Yikes!

A couple black detectives and outgoing detective trainees told me to just keep my head down, do my job, and everything would be okay. Well, here we go. *Okay, bozz, I's b' real gud, suh.* Well, that did not last long.

I worked as hard as I could and I thought as hard as anyone else on the table. One day it happened. I was talking to a black officer who stopped by my desk and my boss exploded.

"Brox, you sit your ass down and get some goddamn work done!"

The visiting officer looked at me and fled the coop.

I responded to him. "You really don't have to talk to me like that."

"You have not done a damn thing since you've been here. I don't need you flapping your lips all the time. Get some cases done."

I looked for help from the veterans, the so-called black veterans. Crickets! I mentally scratched my head, sat myself right down, and got to work like a good boy.

As time went on, he (this redneck) loosened up on me. He started to treat me with dignity. Later, I found out that the ex-Metro guy stood up for me and spoke to my boss. He (my boss) was still an old fart and his neck was still red, but he was manageable. I guess that is what WE all did, was manage.

I worked the auto theft table and burglary and the juvenile table. The time came for the first detective test, and I was having so much fun during my time off that I forgot to study. The results came out. I knew I did not pass due to the white letter sent to my house.

Dear Mr. Brox, you did not receive a passing score on the written portion of the detective's examination.

Okay, I had one more try.

We had a squad meeting with all the detective personnel present. The results of the test were made public. My name was not mentioned as one of Wilshire's fine trainee who passed the exam. The lieutenant, a country boy from Alabama said, "The rest of you dummies better pass the next test or you are outta here." The entire room erupted in laughter. The pressure is on, no quit here!

Some detectives like homicide, some like robbery, I found my niche—Sexual Assault Investigation—the juvenile/sex crimes table. We handled missing juveniles and crimes against children under the age of eighteen. I put my foot into learning and becoming the best investigator possible. I had a great teacher; he was one of the old schoolers, a black man that had been away on illness for some time. He explained how important this position was and how it was not for everybody.

I learned the difference in interviewing someone and interrogating a person. He taught me how to press and how to listen. I was getting it and I was enjoying serving my community again.

A young eighteen-year-old Hispanic girl was sitting in the lobby of the station on a Monday morning waiting for detectives. The officer told me she had been there the entire weekend. I walked out to meet her. She had an eye injury that baffled me. "Ma'am, have you seen a doctor?"

"No, the officers told me to wait for the detectives."

During the interview, she told me the almost unbelievable story of how she was from Mexico, the product of a one-night stand in Jalisco. Her mother brought her to live with the man who fathered her. Her mother left her with this male stranger at ten years old. She had not seen or heard from her mother since. She told me that since she was about eleven, her father had been sexually abusing her almost daily. She told me that she never went to school, never was allowed to leave the apartment that was later found to be ready to be demolished. Her father would come to her side of the bed nightly; they slept together on a dirty stained mattress. The place was as clean as she could keep it. They had no running water and used a hose and a bucket to relive themselves.

I listened for about an hour. I got her treatment for her eye. She explained that her father got drunk and wanted to have sex with her and she refused because he had just vomited all over himself. He then punched her in the face. He passed out and she left. A bus driver allowed her to ride the bus free. She ended up at Santa Monica Police Department and they dropped her off at Wilshire Station.

She produced two Polaroid photos of her and her father at a party. She had on makeup, stockings, and her bra was stuffed. She had a beer bottle turned up drinking it and the other photo her father was kissing her with his tongue in her mouth. The date on the photos indicated the victim was thirteen or fourteen years old.

We put a plan together to go to the apartment to speak with the father and suspected sexual abuser. She told us he had a gun and told her he would use it on her or anyone else. He was a security guard at a Korean bank.

We were not able to locate him at his home, but we called the bank where we thought he worked. He left just before our call. There was a shooting call at an apartment and the suspect was a security guard that matched our suspect. We discovered that our suspect was looking for our victim and shot his own brother in the butt because he claimed his brother was hiding the victim.

He was desperate. I wrote a search warrant for his apartment. As we arrived, our uniformed officers spotted the suspect trying to leave the location. He had bags of clothes and personal items in this vehicle. He was ready to leave for good.

We got into the apartment. It was shocking. Filthy, smelled horrible and the mattress she described was covered by the dirtiest sheet one can imagine. Stained with what appeared to be bodily fluids, secretions, and blood. I found more explicit photos of the victim and the suspect posing as a couple. I recovered the evidence and later found evidence that indicated the victim had at least two abortions. We got search warrants and were able to serve the clinic that matched our evidence. She was told by her father to tell the nurses that her boyfriend had gotten her pregnant.

The clinic kept some of the evidence from the procedure. We had all collected evidence tested against the victim and the suspect. It all matched her father. I interviewed the suspect with the assistance of Spanish speaking officers. He denied all allegations. I interrogated him for some time with a seasoned detective, and he finally admitted to most of the sex crimes and the shooting of his brother, but he called that an accident.

For his crime, he was facing one hundred nine years in prison. He made a plea deal. Forty-five years. He was arrested at the age of thirty-seven. In California, a person convicted of felony sexual assault must serve at least eighty-five percent of their conviction sentence before being eligible for parole.

He will be too damn old to matter.

Some juvenile cases have made a deep impact on me in terms of understanding or *not* understanding human behavior. The two cases shaped who I will become as a protective father, loving husband, champion for children, and those who cannot protect themselves.

I was at my desk when a patrol Lieutenant came into the squad room and informed my boss that a possible kidnapping was in progress. I was the only one working juvenile who was available. It was around noon; most everyone else was at lunch or bullshitting around the station. He told my boss that his patrol guys were en route to a call for service. A distraught mother had called because her husband had their two-year-old son and he (the father) was not going to bring him back unless she reconsidered their pending divorce. No urgency there except the husband was threatening to kill the boy and himself. Well, that elevates the case a bit. My boss told me to go to the scene and report back to him once I had a handle. Now, mind you, I was a detective trainee and relatively new, but I was no dummy. I gathered my things, gun, badge, jacket and notebook. I jumped in our freshly washed black Crown Victoria with tinted windows and sped off to the scene.

I arrived at the scene, a large upscale apartment complex near La Brea and Fairfax. I was informed the mother of the boy was in phone contact with the also distraught father. As I gathered bits and pieces about the parents, it was painfully obvious that there would be no quick solution to this case. By the time I had enough information to call my boss and ask for advice, he was end of watch, gone for the day, on his way home. "Damn, by myself."

I remember in my training that once a detective arrives on the crime scene, the detective is in charge, but I was not a DETECTIVE. I was a trainee. The field lieutenant came to me and said, "Okay, Brox, what are we doing here? Where do you need my guys?" My stomach bubbled; I think I farted, a silent one, the kind that just slips out due to nervousness. I pulled myself together and started acting like I knew what to do.

It turned out, I actually started to get in the resources I needed. I called in units from other divisions because it was change of watch and the father (suspect) was making threats, credible threats. I spoke to him over the phone. The tone of his voice, his threats and the emotional pleas of his demands were serious.

He wanted to meet his ex here, so we sent units there. He fled. He changed the location, we sent units (plain-clothes units) there, he saw them and fled. We were chasing him all over the west side of Los Angeles. He finally told us if he could not have his family, no one would be a family.

I called in the media; we went live on the air. After the commanding officer spoke, I was it! The information officer. I sought the communities help, for the sake and safety of the little boy. We put out the description of the suspect, his vehicle and the clothing of the little boy. I set up a landline, put the number out over the air in hopes to have a sighting to save this family and avoid a tragedy. It was getting to that point.

He spoke to the ex and told her he was going to kill the boy and himself. I asked to get his family to speak to him. They arrived from other parts of the city; they tried to reason with him to leave the child with anyone. I used California Highway Patrol (CHP), Sheriffs, Air Support and Los Angeles City and Los Angeles County lifeguards. We were unable to locate this guy and no one was able to talk to him into sparing the child.

After about six hours of negotiating, pleading over the phone and a city and countywide search of land, sea and air, a frantic call came in to the landline. We heard the worst news possible.

I had several units transport the mother and her entire family to the station. The media was hounding us as we quickly left the scene, heading to the new crime scene. The beach in Malibu. I made sure via the police radio that no one would discuss what we were to discover on the shores of the beach. By the time we arrived on the scene, the media was all over the beach.

Thank God for the Los Angeles County Sheriff's Department creating a crime scene barrier that kept out onlookers. The little boy was found on the beach, near the water's edge, deceased. The witness saw a man leaving the water carrying a child. He watched the man abandon the little body, walk on the parking lot, and enter a vehicle. He heard what he thought was a gunshot. The father was gone, deceased of a single gunshot wound to his head. We had photos of both the suspect and the little boy. It was confirmed; they were the people we fought to save.

I swore and tried to help the helpless, and this child was precious as all children are. The suspect, even if it was the child's father, was a self-centered, egotistical, spoiled brat. He was and is a murderer. He took innocence and snuffed it out because of his uncontrollable jealousy and insecurities yet, I (we) failed to rescue and save this child. This case hurt me, deeply.

ooooo

I returned to the daily grind of juvenile runaway cases, kids disrespecting their parents and the occasional neighborhood pervert case.

Five-foot-eight, one hundred fifty-five pounds, and a real nut bag. He would prowl the neighborhoods just across the street from the station at night, select multi-unit apartment complexes, and toss rocks at the windows until women (fat, skinny, ugly or pretty) would look out. That was when he went to work. His job was flogging the bishop, choking the chicken, and spanking the monkey. Most of the people that made reports described his member as, "a twelve-inch bat" or "a pipe." One woman gave her description and thought he was "putting lotion on his leg." Dang!

We finally caught "Mr. Dick" (as we named him). Previously able to get him convicted on a misdemeanor and caught him on a felony attempt rape and attempt kidnapping of a United States postal worker.

Upon processing him on the assault charges, a strip search was required. Holy shit!

I called my female partner to meet me at the jail. She arrived during the strip search, peered into the jail to see what I was doing, screamed, and then said, "Goddamn, this dude must have been related to Mr. Ed, a distant cousin to Silver, the Lone Ranger's horse." This suspect was relaxed and his penis was dang near at his kneecap. Perhaps he should have been arrested for attempted assault with a deadly ding-a-ling!

He served his time, registered as a sex offender, and moved to Texas.

ooooo

I responded to a case of a young, white nineteen-year-old female from Orange County making allegations that a group of black guys raped her in one of Wilshire's gang areas. She drove down to Los Angeles with friends and had been "partying" with these guys all weekend. Her friends wanted to leave, she wanted to stay. They left her, but she had no money to return home. She refused all medical treatment and did not want to be interviewed without her mother. Her mother responded to the hospital. We spoke very briefly in the lobby. "I don't want some NWA talking to my daughter about her being raped by a bunch of black gang members," she said.

I called my boss and he asked her what she meant. She told him, "A nigger with an attitude." He went off on her and chased her back to the Orange County area.

ooooo

This case still affects me to this day. My partner and I responded to a child abuse call on Washington Avenue. The child, a five-year-old female was scalded in a hot tub of water by the baby sitters boyfriend. We detained him and took him to the station for an interview and depending on what he says in interrogation. This brother (using the term loosely) was a complete dork. He was skinny with a potbelly; he sported a hairstyle that forced us to dub him, "Black Bozo." His crime was no joke.

He admitted drawing a bath for the little girl after his girlfriend went to the store. He explained that the little girl had an accident in her clothes. He was going to have her "bathe herself." He helped her remove her clothes and was upset. She got into the tub and when he returned to check on her, she was sitting in the water and her skin was floating on top of the water.

He dressed her and called his girlfriend who came home. He said his girlfriend saw the girl, skin dripping from underneath her clothes and crying. She called an ambulance, the police and the child's grandparents.

I wanted to strangle this motherfucker right there. But, I had to maintain my composure; I wanted to and I may have cried when I momentarily stepped out of the interview room. I know my partner, a mother of young children, cried. I asked her not to cry because we had a job to do. This beautiful child. I can only imagine how helpless she was.

Her grandparents traveled by bus every day to Sherman Oaks Burn Center—*every day*— to visit their granddaughter. Moved by this case, I wanted to raise money for the family. I set up an account at the only black owned bank I knew of, Broadway Federal Savings. I went to an auto dealership and was able to get them to donate a car for the family to facilitate their daily visits to the hospital. I would visit the little girl weekly at the hospital, sometimes more than weekly and on the weekends. I was not going to quit on this case or this child.

The donations were slowly trickling in. I had to create a way to get more people involved. I presented the case to OJB, a black police officer association. They acted as if they were interested, but the board dragged their feet and took *no* action to create or generate donations. I would not quit. I spoke to businesses, entertainers, and radio stations.

92.3 The Beat was very helpful. They put on a morning breakfast show with John London and the House Party specifically for the little girl and her family. They donated *all* the money raised from the breakfast. With the broadcast, they generated more from the callers and fans of the show.

When I spoke to KJLH, they told me they did not have the funds to give as a donation. They had a softball team who would help in any way they could.

My partner and I put on a benefit softball game with LAPD officers playing against KJLH's team. I had face painting, clowns, and a martial arts demonstration by some of the members of the Karate Kid cast and a K-9 demonstration put on by me and my training group. LAPD K-9 refused our request.

Both events were successful in raising nearly $15,000 for the family and the vehicle.

The case against "Black Bozo" was very upsetting. His conviction was a mere seven years, but the pain and suffering he caused a little girl will last a lifetime. Justice served? Nope!

I had been pretty successful and handled several sexual assault cases in a professional manner. I was able to maintain a very high rate of solving some problematic cases. My reports were very thorough; my interviews with victims were sympathetic yet firm enough to get to the truth. I had the ability to get the truth out of the suspected sex offenders. That I owe to my boss. He pulled something out of me and helped me mold it into a Sexual Assault Investigator.

ooooo

Our unit started to see a pattern of women being sexually assaulted on San Vicente Boulevard. The forth incident caused us to realize we had a rapist on our hands, possibly a serial rapist.

My boss called the Robbery Homicide Division ((RHD), Rape Special. They reviewed our pattern. The lieutenant there was a clean-cut old school veteran who wore a flat top haircut, white short-sleeve shirt and a black tie every day. He called my boss and me to his office. He told us that he liked some of the cases they had reviewed and he was confident I could handle the case. He looked at me and mentioned that I was young, clean cut and a sharp dresser. He went on to say that one day he would like to see me at RHD and this case may be the case to be judged by, "So don't fuck it up."

I took off headfirst into this case. I re-interviewed all the victims and realized there were so many similarities that we were dealing with the same suspect, a serial rapist. His description was somewhat consistent, varying on height, weight and clothing. Some of the commands were slightly different, but the thing that was exact on was that he smelled so bad. His smell was described as almost chemical like but with rotting wet garbage. A few of the victims said that days after the assault, his smell was still in their apartments.

I thought, *A homeless person?* He was a large black man, heavy mustache, unkempt bushy afro and of course, a strong, foul, body odor.

I requested prints to be taken by our specialist at each residence apartment scene. No lifts, yet he was not described as wearing gloves.

I ordered a Department of Justice (DOJ)/Thomas Guide map run of all the sex registrants within a one-square-mile area. The two boxes that arrived from DOJ contained computer generated runs. Hundreds of pages. So much work and research that I took it home with me. My wife helped me look for similarities in the Method of Operation.

Meanwhile, uniformed officers found a guy asleep in a broken down car. He was a sex offender, but they did not arrest or detain him. He had recently been paroled from prison after spending twenty-two years in prison for a rape and robbery conviction.

I found someone that leaped off the pages of the DOJ computer runs. It was the same person that was sleeping in the car, found by the uniform officers. I pulled his conviction case. I studied it very closely and found that his MO and statements to his victims in his conviction was the exact same as in our cases.

In his conviction, he approached lone females as their backs were turned, told them not to turn around or he would stab or shoot them. Forced them back into their apartments, tied up his victims using their own clothing and sexually assault them. He would finally tell them that he was watching them and not to call the police or anyone before thirty minutes after he is gone.

This has to be the same person. The only difference in the previous conviction was no foul order. However, his mother's house was less than three city blocks from each of the current victims and less than a mile from his previous victims. We watched his mother's house and he never went there.

I came up with an idea to have his parole officer call his mother to tell her there was a job for him. She said she would try, but he was not living at her house and has not stayed there after his release due to some family issues.

We set up a perimeter at the parole office and we got the signal that he was in the office. We entered the building and *damn*, we could smell him from the moment we got into the building.

I got him back to the office. Despite my best efforts, the efforts of my partner and my boss, he denied any and all allegations. I know it's him, but I may have jumped the gun. I was able to get a one-year parole hold on him for not living at the address he was paroled to. Off to Chuckwalla State Prison.

I needed to get something on this. I got a court order to get his DNA. I ran a match with each victim and their personal belongings that came in contact with the suspect. In one of the victim's cases, her young son was home during the assault. The suspect tied him up and placed him in the bathtub. I called Wilshire's ALPO (area latent print officer). This officer was good, better than the specialist that first came on the scene. He asked questions and wanted a walk-through of what took place and *bam!* He found a partial palm print in the bathroom where the victim's son was placed.

Within ten months of the suspect's detention, I had this monster. His prints were compared to those lifted in the bathroom. It was a match. The DNA came back a match to all but one victim (a story in itself).

On a Saturday morning, a uniformed officer and I raced to Blythe, California, and served an arrest warrant on this evil man.

He was not surprised to see me. "Hello, Detective Brox. I knew you would not give up or quit."

We went to trial. He represented himself better than any public defender would have done. But, he was up against science, angry women, and a young detective trainee who swore to protect and serve. He received one hundred thirty years. He will rot in prison. And, for three years, he sent Christmas cards to me at the station.

ooooo

I have handled volumes of juvenile and sexual assault investigations as a trainee. The system of preparing trainees to be detectives helped me in so many ways. I have handled crimes against children, terrible acts of violence and less than human behavior. I worked to rescue the helpless and serve the needy.

I saw the devil himself prey on a seven-year-old little girl whose mother was not at her apartment complex to greet her. This monster gain the trust of this little angel with bubble gum then sexually assaulted her behind a trash dumpster. When captured, he would not look my partner or me in the eyes while he confessed his sins.

This creep, who broke into a woman's house, surprised her upon her return from buying groceries to feed her family. The rapist covered her head with a towel and secured it with her son's necktie. He sexually assaulted her repeatedly. He stayed in her house for hours, only to be captured still inside her house, hiding under a couch. His excuse? Her boyfriend was in the military and pointed a gun at him on a bus. Crazy SOB! She was single and had no boyfriend or man in her life in over twelve years. She suffered from depression for a number of years. The thought and preparation to testify in court terrified her. Two days prior to the preliminary hearing, she tried to calm her nerves and overdosed on her prescribed depression medication. We prosecuted and convicted this animal without a victim. No victim in any stage of the court proceedings with the help of Proposition 115. The jury was instructed that the absence of a victim or witness should have no bearing on the facts of this case. They were advised only that the victim was unavailable. This case was the first of its kind (other than a homicide) in California. He will never see the outside of a prison in this life.

One of my last cases was an illustration of parental greed and chasing fame at all cost. The uniform desk officer came to our table and told my partner and me that a young boy came running into the station, shirtless, screaming that a man tried to rape him.

I responded to the desk and saw this shirtless black teenager, maybe fifteen or sixteen years old, very slim build, very dark skin with fresh red scratches and what appeared to be a bite mark on his back. There was also a clothed black male adult, tall about six-foot-two, sweating heavily and ranting about just giving the boy a haircut. He was detained at my request.

The young victim told us that he and his mom met this man at the mall a few weeks prior. He told them he was a talent scout for movies and television. He gave them a half sheet of paper, told them to fill it out and if they were interested in auditioning to put their contact numbers down and he would get back to them. They filled out the paper right there and gave it back to the man.

Within two days, this man called and asked for the victim. The victim and his mother were the only people living in their home. They talked on the phone and he convinced the mother to allow the boy to visit him, alone at his apartment.

During the visit, the man told the victim he needed a haircut and convinced the boy to remove his shirt. While cutting the victim's hair, he (now the suspect) used his bare free hand to act as if he was removing hair from the boy's upper and lower body. At one point, the suspect ran his finger between the victim's buttocks. The victim only moved as a gesture that he was not okay or comfortable.

The suspect moved behind the seated victim and tried to kiss or lick the victim's back. The victim tried to jump away from the grasp of the suspect and was scratched on both sides of his shoulders. The scratches traveled down the boys back.

The victim's mother arrived at the station and gave us a copy of the paper they filled out. It was a very unprofessional document. It looked as if someone typed it and the paper was off line and the sheet was uneven at its tear. The lines were name, height, weight, age, eye color, and school. There was a parent's signature line with the word "authorization" spelled incorrectly.

The mother told us she trusted the man because she thought she heard about this opportunity from other parents at Crenshaw High School.

During the interrogation with the suspect, he held onto the story that he has placed kids (boys only) in commercials. He told us he had been at Crenshaw, Inglewood, and Los Angeles High Schools passing out flyers and he had several clients. This alarmed us based on his admissions and the victim's story of his ordeal.

I had our School Car (they work our juvenile/sexual assault table) contact each school and inform the administration that a predator may have been in contact with their male student population. Several cards were left at each school with the instructions to be discrete in notifying the parents and potential victims. Within a few weeks, six more young black boys and their parents came to our station reporting similar contact with this same suspect. Four of the six boys reported they were involved with oral or anal sex with the suspect in hopes to get into the entertainment business. One of the parents allowed the suspect to spend the night at their home over a weekend in her son's bedroom. That is where this fifteen-year-old victim performed oral copulation on the suspect and the suspect performed oral copulation on the victim as well. All the parents were black, single mothers.

We were able to get a search warrant and arrest warrant for this predator. We arrested him at his home and found information that he had been in Oakland, California, and San Francisco, California. We notified Northern and Southern California agencies. We held a press conference to warn the public and seek closure for potential victims.

Years later, I would receive a subpoena to testify in a hearing before a parole board. The law allows testimony from law enforcement and victims for inherently dangerous felons.

This clown and booty bandit was about to be released back into society. Not if I had anything to do with it.

ooooo

It was my final attempt at the detective examination. Forget just passing, I had to score high enough to be on a published list of detective candidates. At that time, normally the first eleven bands were published. Those folks were a shoe-in to make detective.

I arrived at Hollywood High School early on a Saturday morning with hundreds of officers from all over the city. This was the only place large enough to administer the test. I was serious and focused; my career depended on this final test of my knowledge of department policy and procedure. Standing in line, seeing people I have not seen in years, it appeared I was the only person taking this seriously.

"Hey, Brox, how have you been?" a good person from the 77th Division asked. I nodded, but did not verbally respond. "Damn, brother, loosen up. It is not that serious." For me it was.

I sat down and received instructions. I studied really hard for this test. I was ready for any department policy and procedural questions.

"You may now open your test booklets."

The first question on the examination was something like: What are the call signs for the on-duty underwater dive team commanding officer?

What the fuck?

Well, one question wrong. Despite the deflating start, I passed the test and was promoted to the rank of Detective I. I was transferred to West Valley Division Detectives, Reseda, California, in the San Fernando Valley.

Culture shock. That is how I am going to describe my transition from the "real Los Angeles" to this very upscale region with its own crimes and problems

Problems...well that was apparent the day I walked into the squad room. I was dressed to kill, sharp as a tack, cleaner than a desert bone, I was trying to be impressive. No one noticed. This sea of white men with white shirts, tight ass pants and big clunky "Buster Brown" shoes like a bus driver would wear.

White guys, no brothers...wait, in the distance I saw this old black man, dressed like a broke cowboy. As I got closer, he needed some lotion, ashy and dry. Not only in his appearance but his personality (at first). This was my boss. He was a veteran; an ex-Metro unit. He worked the mounted (officers of horseback) in his younger years, which was obviously a number of years past.

He was the boss Detective III over the auto investigations. He told me that if I was going to work his table, I did not need to come to work looking like a pimp. *Okay, he's got jokes*, I thought. *Maybe this guy is not so bad after all.* I returned the next and every day dressed appropriately for an auto theft detective—jeans and collared shirts and "Buster Brown" type shoes. Clothing and shoes I did not mind getting a bit oily.

He turned out to be a very good brother and friend. However, he kind of allowed and accepted the covert unfair treatment that I know he faced in a police department that he struggled through in the early 1970s.

One day, he and I were in our unmarked detective vehicle. It was broken down, did not look much like a police car. We were driving in an exclusive neighborhood near Woodland Hills. We heard a radio call. "10 A89, possible 459 (Burglary) suspects, two male blacks in a tan Chevy with slightly tinted windows, last seen east on Ventura Boulevard."

As good, alert detectives with skill and dedication, we started looking for and keeping our eyes open for the burglary suspects as we were right in the same area. Next thing we knew, two black and white patrol vehicles had their red and blue lights on us.

"Driver, get out of the car!"

What the fuck? We were the burglary suspects. We were looking for ourselves—the two male black burglary suspects. No wonder we did not see them, we didn't have a mirror. Safely and without sudden movements, we complied with their PA assisted orders. How embarrassing, on this major street—Ventura Boulevard. We knew better than to act with non-compliance; with these scary ass, young white police officer and two giant black burglary suspects, if we got shot, that would be easy for them to explain.

We got out as ordered and once they figured out we had badges and guns just like them, they lowered their guns and brushed us off. I looked at my boss who had a look on his face as if to say, *Here we go again.*

"Nothing has changed in society and law enforcement, huh?" I said.

I think some things have changed, like hanging, whipping and burning people of color for simply looking at other people (well at least a little in the last fifty-five to sixty years). Working in this new environment is going to be a challenge, a challenge that I am up to.

I worked the auto table with my boss for three or four months. They changed my assignment to burglary. My new boss was a very tall and surprisingly well-dressed white man, older but with a continual smile on his face. He seemed to be genuinely a happy man. He was very pleasant and could sing. He sung like a brother in the tenor section of the Missionary of Hope Second First AME Episcopal Baptist Christian church choir.

He was fair and honest and wanted to serve the community with respect and dignity. He had a great sense of humor and laughed heartily all the time. He ate his lunch at two places and two places only—Melody's and Los Fuentes Mexican restaurants.

One day a very wealthy person was at the station screaming at me because he was frustrated that his home was broken into. He was extremely rude and critical of the efforts of West Valley Detectives. He asked to speak to my supervisor.

My boss took over the conversation. The homeowner asked for another detective to be assigned to the case. My boss asked him where this request was when this crime first occurred. My boss told him no and gave me a compliment that I will never forget. Not knowing me that long, I didn't know if he was just saying these things to get the guy to calm down or if he was being honest.

I told the boss thank you for the compliment. He told me I deserved it. He had done his background check on me with Wilshire Division. Wilshire had great things to say about me and I showed no difference in my short time and work at West Valley. He also told me that he knew of my desire was to work sex crimes. "Be patient, my friend, good things come to those who wait."

I worked hard at this table, my boss retired and they brought in some doofus to replace him. That did not go well. I went to the lieutenant and asked to work sex crimes. He looked at me and told me he did not think I was ready to work sex crimes. "You need a little more training working other cases." Now there was a trainee, a white female with less time on the job and about five months in detectives working sex crimes. I suggested to someone that I go and ask about that. "Man, leave that alone. Pick your battles. This should not be one of them."

Somehow, my desire to speak to the big boss got back to him and he called me into his office to explain his decision. He told me he did not have to explain anything to me as he assigned his personnel as he saw fit. However, it was his intention to put me in sex crimes, but the timing had to be right. Oops, okay!

A few weeks or so later, I was moved to the sex crimes unit. There was drama going on and it was pretty racy. The old ass Detective II was working with the female trainee—a very nice looking, outgoing young shapely officer. The Detective II, as I was told, started to have "feelings" for the trainee. I did notice he had pet names for her and was seen bringing juice and snacks to her desk frequently.

He was acting like a pussy whipped sugar daddy, but he was not getting any special attention or booty from her. She was cordial to everyone, but this no-game loser took her professionalism the wrong way and got the wrong idea. It was like she was special to him.

I heard and it was substantiated that he and this trainee were out of town for an investigation and this old ass, no game, no swag, ugly broke married man with children told her, "I have feelings for you and I think I love you."

Well, that apparently freaked the shit out of her and she called from where they were, asking for help. Once they got back, he was transferred out of the division and retired shortly thereafter before they could fire his ass for sexual harassment.

I guess this was the moment that my lieutenant was waiting for. Now I was working sex crimes with her. I tell you what; she was one of the best detective partners I ever had.

She was married with a young child, funny, goofy, hardworking, professional and laughed at my corny jokes.

She and I put a bunch of perverts and rapists in jail. We took every one of our cases seriously. We enjoyed our job, provided professional service and had fun doing it.

One of our cases of sexual assault turned into uncontrollable laughter as she and I was working on a juvenile sexual assault arrest. Well this fourteen-year-old girl, about five-foot-eight, one hundred sixty to one hundred seventy pounds accused and convinced her mother that their family friend, a fourteen-year-old boy, five-foot-one, eighty-one pounds, forced her to orally copulate him. Yeah, right. Her story did not "measure up."

So my partner tells this, not so little girl, "Hold on, honey." My partner left and returned with a fifteen-inch ruler. "So what you are telling us is that this little shit of a boy's "wiener" is longer than fifteen inches?" I almost fell out of my chair.

The girl's mother, who was present in the interview, gave her daughter a "bitch, please" look.

She finally admitted the act between the two of them was consensual. She made up the story to hide the fact that her clothes were soiled. She did not want her mom to wonder why she changed. Her mom asked why she changed garments and the lies just flowed.

Little man was released from Juvenile Hall before someone got a hold of him.

ooooo

My partner and I worked a case where this short, black midget like, Olympic sprinter want-to-be raped and beat up his roommate. This guy was shorter than a midget on his knees.

We got some information as to his current whereabouts. He was going to pick up a check on Ventura Boulevard. My partner and I, being the professionals we were, included patrol resources and other detectives in our attempts to capture the suspect.

Everyone was in place, all our equipment, my partner in a mini skirt, high heel shoes and a police raid jacket walked across Ventura Boulevard toward a mostly glass building

This little jackass saw us approaching. He pushed open the door and took off running toward freedom. I was in pretty good shape; I gave chase on foot. My partner was not as fast as I was. As she was trying to broadcast the direction, she lost her radio, kicked off her five-inch pumps and kept running. The suspect jumped a wall, at least ten feet high—dang! He ran through a back yard with two large Akita dogs. They barked and snarled at us. Sorry-ass watch dogs. We were the good guys.

The perimeter was set. I looked at my partner, her hair flying everywhere, her stockings were ripped to shreds and now were dangling around her feet and ankles. I started cracking up. She told me she was running behind me after she lost her radio and was broadcasting using my radio that clipped to my belt just over my butt.

The K-9 Unit found this little speedster hiding in an algae-filled Jacuzzi. We took him to get medical treatment and he wanted to fight against court ordered DNA and blood samples.

Down he went to the floor. My partner was straddling his chest with a skirt on. He got a quick peek. She started laughing and called him a sick, perverted little bastard. I miss her. She was great to work with. She made this job fun.

ooooo

People say money (or the love of money) is the root of all evil. I have to agree. My family and I needed more money or a winning lottery ticket.

I was in a city where a bunch of people with money lived. They look to law enforcement officers to protect their homes, businesses, events and families. We call this moonlighting, working off duty. The fees can be staggering, sometimes topping $100 per hour. The department wants their officers and employees to have work permits for outside work. However, it takes a while to process the permits. If your potential client wants your services without delay, one has a decision to make. I often made the wrong decisions. But, the money was so easy.

Working for entertainers and sports figures was very, very lucrative. When that dried up, officers and I looked at local nightclubs, bars and restaurant type establishments. The pay was good, but not mind blowing. An officer would normally make $30 to $35 per hour standing in a parking lot or standing in front of the door of a nightclub.

I got caught on a few times without a work permit and was suspended. I had to leave that easy money alone.

I interviewed for several jobs to advance to the level of Detective II. No takers.

I received a call from RHD, Robbery Homicide Rape Special. The old lieutenant had not forgotten about me. I had more experience now and I was a shoe-in for the promotion and this coveted position, I thought.

I took the interview at RHD. I answered the question like I have never been a detective in my entire career. In other words,

I bombed, I stunk up the joint, I was a disappointment. Not my words but the words of the lieutenant who called me after the selections. I was not one of the selections. He told me I was arrogant and acted as if I was the best thing going. He went in on me that RHD did not need arrogance, they simply needed the best and I was not prepared. My interview came across as an arrogant, know nothing table detective. He told me good luck in my career and to use this as a learning experience. I crawled from underneath my desk and to my car after that phone call. Well, there goes that raise.

I had an opportunity to work on loan at Internal Affairs. Most would say that this assignment was the road to promotion. Another chance? This sounds good to me. I applied and got the loan. I was assigned to Mr. Internal Affairs II. He would later become an assistant chief of this agency. He was very good at his job, meticulous and knowledgeable. But this was not for me, so I faked like I was enjoying myself.

I really disliked the treatment I received from the troops. Especially the black officers and detectives. My IA partner and trainer, Mr. Internal Affairs II, would show up for an investigation at stations citywide. Some officers I knew and came up with in the ranks looked at me and turned away. Many did not speak. I would occasionally here "Uncle Tom."

Cool, I wondered what I did. Who did I offend? Was I an Uncle Tom for working as an investigator who looks into possible police misconduct?

I looked hard at myself and decided, fuck them! I am trying to better myself and make a better and easier living for my family.

My partner was the man. He seemed to get the special cases, the high interest cases. One was that racist detective involved in the OJ trial. I am going to leave that one alone.

ooooo

One story that shines above all others while I was at IA was the case when the other Mr. Internal Affairs (a Lieutenant II) was suspected of having unlawful sex with a minor. It was a rumor at first and was most likely over.

However, my partner and trainer told me we had to attend a meeting. The meeting was with a deputy chief who informed us that Lieutenant II, Mr. Internal Affairs was just arrested for his continual unlawful relationship with an under aged girl. This balding clown acted as if he was God's gift to police work. He could do no wrong. He got caught with his pants down, literally.

Working at IA opened my eyes to the unfair treatment to employees in this Mickey Mouse system that has not changed since the 1920s. The system of reporting and adjudication is arbitrary, punitive and has no sense of fairness.

It appears that black officers and employees are more likely to be punished more severely for similar treatment than whites. One of the major problems is favor. If you have favor (your relatives were high ranking or highly respected members of LAPD), your penalties are often reduced drastically or may be no punishment at all. However, for black officers there is no favor. We have no power, we don't have the people in high places that are willing to stand up and intervene (at least the few that are there will not help).

My suggestion has always been, have all matters of misconduct and uses of force investigated and adjudicated by an independent firm or organization without ties to the city of Los Angeles. All levels of discipline, punishment and suggestions of termination should be handled away from the police department and the city of Los Angeles. Get away from the police commission; there is favor in that the mayor is responsible for appointments of its members. Give the power and control over public servants to the intelligent and educated public.

CHAPTER SEVEN

Biggest Mistake of My Career

I should have listened to my wife.

I took another round of Detective II interviews with Central Traffic Detectives (CTD), Pacific Division, and West Los Angeles Division. I did much better on all three. I received calls from Pacific and CTD, offering me the Detective II position.

I went home and discussed it with my wife, my best friend. She strongly suggested that I NOT take the CTD job. She gave me her reasons and she made a lot of sense, but my dumb ass did not listen. The next day, I accepted the position at CTD. *Big mistake!* Definitely the biggest mistake of my career and possibly my life!

History is a teacher and people who love you can help you make decisions based on history.

The new boss at CTD was a very close family friend. (Never work for or with family.) Shit, she was a friend of my family. I guess that was close enough. Stupid me.

My wife saw the dangers years before the events even happened. I wish she could have done that with the lottery! On the first day of my new assignment as a Detective II supervisor, I got called out to a traffic crime scene (no such thing I was told).

Before I arrived at the scene, I was told a fatal auto vs. pedestrian hit and run took place. I looked around and there was no one there except one P2 traffic officer, sitting in her vehicle writing her report.

Cars were driving by, crushing auto debris such as headlight fragments, parking light fragments, and a license plate. I asked the officer who broke down "my" scene without my being on the scene. She told me that there is no scene. "We don't do that here." So let me get this straight. A car kills a pedestrian, fled the scene, left portions of the only car involved, there were skid marks and there was no crime scene established? I mumbled, "It's not going to be that way for long." Mistake #2.

My boss told me, "I need you to be strong and stand up to these good ol' boys. Don't let them run over you; they will try."

Central Traffic Division was one of the department's last strong holds for the good ol' boys club. CTD Detective had investigators P3+1 as their detectives. They were old time white guys with a lot of time on the job. All of them never left CTD after their probation spent the entire career as CTD AI, TE, Motor officers and now P3+1 investigators. This is all they know.

The next day, I met with my friend, I mean, boss and explained to her the issue with the crime scenes. She suggested I come up with training to address it with All Central Bureau and CTD. I made a simple copy from a homicide manual and added the importance of evidence. She looked it over, made a few corrections, and blessed it. I made visits to all Central Bureau Divisions and addressed my concerns with CTD Watch Commanders to share with the troops. Mistake #3.

The following week was divisional photo day. All CTDs took a panoramic photo to be displayed in the hallway of CTD. A few days later, the photo was on the wall. I took a gander. My image on the panoramic photo was defaced, eyes torn out and face almost scribbled out. I was a brand new person, hardly knew anyone and this is how I am treated, within three weeks.

I just could not get anything right. It seemed as if the people in the office hated me, including the other detective supervisors who were black females accept one milk toast dork of a white guy.

All of the guys were lazy, scammers, taking money from the city and cared nothing about its residents. We had a red-faced fat guy who seemed to be the ringleader, a very skinny balding follower who acted like he was the expert but would not bust a grape.

There was this desk officer, an older Hispanic guy, heavy set with bad knees. He looked like he should be at home with great grandchildren.

Our clerk typist was an ex-beauty queen's stunt double. She was very nice, but could never be at work on time. She loved money, nice things, and flashy cars.

One of the laziest, good-for-nothing, but making excuses for not being at work, I have ever been around. This guy, who was a Detective I, claimed to have a duty related injury for every portion of his short body. If there was ever anyone that did not deserve a paycheck, it was this bum. But, he knew how to "milk" the system. He had a golden stool and he did not shy away from telling supervision, if they pushed him, he would call his attorney and file a lawsuit. Call his doctors and go off IOD for several months. He was a pitiful excuse for a man.

Our Captain, a stocky white guy who had a speech impediment—he stuttered—was something else.

I recall just having a terrible time in the office. I had my own desk; I would lean back in my chair as I would talk to other detectives, other agencies and be on hold for investigative material. My boss would tap me on the shoulder and say, "I need to see you in my office when you are done." I was being reprimanded for unprofessional conduct in the workplace. I asked why, what did I do. "You were on a personal phone call, leaning back smiling and have a good ol time while on the clock." I asked if she was listening to my phone calls. She said she was not, it just looked like you were on a personal call and the employees were complaining.

I walked in one day, and she asked, "Where is your employee?" I just walked in to start my shift. I had no idea. She told me he was upstairs cooking barbecue for the Metro Division. "He needs to be down here working cases." She told me to have him return to his desk.

I did what I was told. He came back, face red as a firecracker. He was the old ringleader of the old school crew, perhaps the one who marked up my photo. She told me to write a "comment card" reminding him that he was to check with his supervisor if he was to be away from his workplace for an extended period of time. Mind you, he started his shift at 6:00am, as well as my boss. I start at 8:30am.

I wrote the card, let her approve it before serving it on him, she approved it and I served it on him, I really did not think it took all that. He got up and took the card to the Captain's Office. A few hours later, I was called to the Captain's Office.

My stuttering Captain lit into me. He scolded me for being so petty with one of the division's most senior members. I said, wait a minute Captain, I was told to do this by my boss, and approved by her before I gave it to him. I asked to have her vouch for me and my claims.

She came to the office and straight lied. She told the captain that the comment card was my idea and she warned me that it may cause backlash, but went with it anyway.

The captain ripped up the comment card right in front of me. "Brox, li li li li listen, you are going to have a rough time her unless u u u u u you learn real quick how to ma ma ma amama manage." I could not believe she ran me over with the bus.

I was driving to the station on a summer morning. I was in my personal SUV. I had my windows down, listening to music when this guy stopped his car, got out of his vehicle and started to walk away, blocking lanes in downtown LA. I raised my hand in disbelief that he was so rude.

He looked at me with my hands raised. He started walking toward my passenger window. I have a briefcase with my on duty weapon in side. It was on the seat next to the opened window where he sat. He asked me, "What's your fucking problem?" He looked at my left hand and I was holding my off duty two-inch Smith and Wesson .38 revolver inside *my* car that he just walked up to. He backed away, the traffic maneuvered around his car. I left.

As soon as I got to the station, I told my boss. "I had to pull my gun out on a crazy man that walked up to my car talking shit." Her response was "Okay, let's see if he comes in to make a complaint."

The next thing I knew, my boss ensured that criminal report of assault with a deadly weapon was made on me. I was named as the suspect due to the allegation by this crazy dude who approached me as I was sitting in *my* car minding *my* own business.

I was ordered to a board of rights (an LAPD kangaroo court system) and I was suspended. This board of rights is a joke, there are rules, but they do not apply if your name is on the radar. The case was submitted to the District Attorney's Office. I thought this was it, my wife was terrified, and I was too. I had two little girls, children to care for, feed, educate, and mentor and a mortgage to pay.

Remember, this person is / was my FAMILY FRIEND. How can anyone treat family like that? She was not finished with me.

I survived; the DA chose not to prosecute me, Lack of corpus. That means that the case lacked elements to establish the crime or charge. I thank God for an independent review of the *facts*.

I pressed on and had good cases with my subordinates. I carried cases as well as supervised. (There should be separation of work and responsibility of supervision and subordinate.)

ooooo

One case, I was on the trail of this guy who killed a lady and her child that was in a stroller. He left the scene and was on the loose. We held a news release to get the public's help in finding this hit and run murderer. Along with one of my investigators, we tracked down leads, spoke to informants, and were able to locate the suspect in the valley working at a body shop. We interrogated him at Van Nuys division. He confessed and told us all the details and where to find his car that was about to be repaired.

I called my boss to update her and told her some of the details of his confession. The next morning she called a press conference. We were all standing there to thank the public for their assistance. Then, she started actually giving details of the suspect's confession. We have not presented the case to the DA's office yet. She was just talking. I tugged on her jacket and whispered, "Don't give away our case and evidence." She looked back at me and continued.

She called me into her office and closed the door. She called me every name in the book. She told me she gave me this job and if it were not for her, I would not be a Detective II. She told me don't ever try to embarrass her again. She reminded me that *she was the officer in charge*, not me. I still did not get the hint that I needed to go.

I had a few great cases and some not so great ones. I was assigned a misdemeanor hit and run with property damage only. I went on vacation. The victim of the hit and run complained I did not do anything for his case.

I was given a notice to correct deficiencies. I was furious; I went to the captain and asked to be transferred. He denied it. I placed my name on the transfer request. I left there and went to another division.

My former boss was vindictive. She wrote a "Special Rating" for me and I had not been at her division in nearly 8 months. This "Special Rating" was to downgrade me from the rank of Detective II. She used the same incident that was on the notice to correct, so I was being punished for the same thing, twice. It worked; the Chief of Police approved it. (She worked for the chief where she was a sergeant.) I thought an employee could not be disciplined for the same incident twice. Not done yet.

One of her hench*women* called my new lieutenant and told him there was an investigation on me. I was shocked that it was for the same incident again. I looked for help. I went to the place I thought could help me, OJB, Oscar Joel Bryant Foundation. My rep (the best "man" on this job) went to them and asked for the services of the attorney I was paying for through the organization for the betterment of the black police officer.

These house Negroes denied me what I have paid for over the years. They told me that if I put myself in the position, it would not look good pitting two black employees against one another.

I asked for the organization to cancel my almost twenty-year membership. They gladly did.

I went to the only people that had an employee's best interest. The Los Angeles Police Protective League, they were very helpful to me, I went to La Lay (Hispanic Organization) they helped. I sought out the suggestion of several well-respected black leaders within the department; they turned their back on me. I then went to several white leaders. They were helpful with suggestions, attorney services, policy and procedure, and support.

This investigation took me to the board of rights again. My rep and I went on the defensive. Together we investigated, pulled documents, and fought within the policy and procedures of the LAPD system.

On a rainy day, my rep and I arrived at CTD to gather discovery documents in preparation for my defense. We both were dressed for the weather. We were clean, sharp, and regal looking. We both had on Fedoras, long trench coats and carried briefcases. We walked into the detective room and everyone looked and stared.

My former boss asked why we were there. I did not speak. My rep said, "We are here to get discovery."

She told my rep, "I can get what you need. Wait in the lobby and I will get the documents."

"Bitch, we work here too, we are not citizens, we are police employees," I said to myself.

I recall seeing other people, auditors, defense reps come into the office and she never told anyone else (mostly white people) to wait outside. My rep said that He had the right to get the documents. "Why are you treating Brox like this?" he asked her. She got really pissed off and left the office.

The next thing I know, a white sergeant and a white lieutenant came to the office and asked us to come to the captain's office with them. She told the captain that we were trying to intimidate her and her employee's with our presence. I can't make this stuff up folks.

The board of rights started and my rep called her to the stand.

"How did we get here? Are you and Brox and his family friends?"

"No," she responded.

I could not breathe.

"Are you Brox's daughter's godmother?"

Before she could fix her mouth to lie, the board interrupted the line of questioning.

Long story short, she told the board that she had a perchance meeting with the Chief of Police and he asked her to do a complete investigation on me. That was it!

I was found guilty of that I had already been disciplined for, rated for and now given a forty-four-day suspension and demotion for the rank of detective.

I was flattened, I was broken, heart broken. A longtime friend, a sister in description of being very close to my real family, shared family dinners, Christmas, Thanksgiving, our children's birthdays, my middle child's godmother. We traveled to other countries together. I was a pallbearer at her mother's funeral. I could not believe this. She went there. Another black employee turned on another black employee.

She hurt my wife deeply. My wife considered her a sister. They were inseparable. I hurt my wife. I let her and my kids down. I felt less than a man. How could this happen? If I had only listened to my wife at the beginning, none of this would have happen. I am so sorry.

I did figure out why this happened. I heard from a reliable source that my former boss was getting the business (as I did) from the good ol' boys at CTD. She needed someone to deflect the issues and focus on as she had plans to be promoted and any adverse employee relationships would hurt her chances to promote.

To my former boss and friend: YOU allowed this police shit to come between us. I can forgive, but the hurt is so deep, so violent, and engraved in my memory that I just cannot forget. The bond we had *was* special. That is shattered and cannot be fixed. There was room for all of us within LAPD. I cannot figure out why you wanted me crushed so badly. I recently saw you and you told me, "I love you." I wondered if you really meant that because you never reached out to me to try to explain what the fuck happened.

CHAPTER EIGHT

I Will Forever Be Changed

Well, a number of my coworkers and ex-subordinates gave me a "demotion" party, the first in LAPD history. There was not a face like mine in the house. The people that supported me during this time were and still are amazing.

I was to be without work, a paycheck for four weeks, and out of work for forty-four days. I was not a rich man, I needed help. For the first time in my life, I was temporarily out of work and one or two paychecks away from losing my house. My children depended on me to provide them with food, clothing and shelter. This was really bad. I needed help. I dropped to my knees and asked God to help me help my family.

I was at home about to quit; I searched to see what the insurance policy offered. The phone rang, I answered, it was a voice from heaven. One of my white detective friends from West Valley.

"Hey, buddy, hang in there. Do you need anything?"

I responded with a quivering voice, "Yes I do need help for me and my family."

"Hey, Brox, I understand," he paused. Then, he told me he had a security business and could assign me to a couple of job sites that I could work if I needed to. "Brox, work as much as you need."

I went to work—three jobs, seven days a week. God will provide!

Never got a call from anyone from Wilshire, but everyone knew my situation.

Remembering my conversation with the old brother at 77th desk.

I was now a P3, a uniformed officer. The technology has changed so much that it was impossible for me to go out into the field as a training officer. I worked the front desk for almost eight years.

I tried several times to get my detective position back, to no avail. I had a fitness hearing with this captain who I once was her training officer. She was very judgmental over the top in her assessment of me being promoted. She not only did not support me getting my position back, she wrote in her document that she did not think I should be a police officer anymore.

That is truly funny seeing that I was being judged by a less than moral, sex crazed low life that will do anything to be promoted. One year at the Police Olympics, this same person who was chosen to be a commanding officer, in charge of leading men and women with morality and character was a group toy to a bunch of very tall and dark men. These guys ran through her like water in a canyon. But she judged me? #stankhoethatnobodyknows?

I stayed in my demoted rank, worked hard to keep my anger and frustrations to myself. I felt victimized and singled out by a power driven black woman and her enabler, the Chief of Police, another black man.

I went to speak to my commanding officer at Foothill, a Hispanic man with character. He told me that the chief was not going to allow me to get my position back regardless of the policy and procedures were. He did however; allow me to work in detectives. Word spread that I was going back to detectives. Several non- black detectives and detective supervisors asked me if I were interested in working their tables. I was floored and flattered. Some people have hearts.

I eventually accepted a position in a special unit. We had a bunch of fun serving the community again. Not the end of the story. I took a detectives test, passed and prepared for the interview.

I had a panel of three—a black lieutenant, a white lieutenant, and a black civilian. The questions were very basic and simple. I answered each question with experience and how my decisions would impact the community, the employees and the department textbook. I felt pretty good about those answers. However, the black lieutenant asked about my demotion. Do I stay with the department and military line? "I made some mistakes" or tell the truth and how I felt. I chose the latter. I explained that I accepted my predicament and moved on. WRONG ANSWER. Here comes the retaliation.

In our civil service point system, you get one point for every five year of service. I was sitting on twenty-three years of service.

So, just by showing up, I got four plus point off the bat. When I received my score in the mail after my overall ranking. I almost fainted.

Overall score of 72. My raking of over three hundred candidates was two hundred ninety-eight, the guy who ranked one point lower than I did walked out of interview before finishing. (Verified) A 72, for a person who was a Detective Trainee for nearly four years, a Detective in four different locations throughout the city, worked Internal Affairs and a Detective Supervisor. I know I did well on that interview, I called my attorney.

The following day, we met with the City's Personnel Department's Commanding Officer. My attorney and personnel listened to my interview. They scheduled me for another interview with a new board, three captains. The same set of questions and basically, I gave the same responses. I got a new score, 104.

My attorney loved it. He used the department's original interview and the re-interview and system of promotion as illustrations of continued retaliation and unfair labor practices against me by LAPD management and the city of Los Angeles.

They settled out of court with the understanding that I would be given back the position of Detective and I would have to earn back the Detective II upgrade. We agreed. I knew if I was to take interviews with people who were fair and judged me not by what some egotistical, power hungry punitive former chief suggested. I took one interview for Detective II and was selected.

I worked hard for those Valley commanding officers that help me along the way. Those that gave me the opportunity to show

how I can lead with genuine care for the community first and reverence for the law.

I soon applied for a Detective III position and after two interviews, I was selected by a core of commanding officers in the valley that judged me on my work, leadership and commitment to service. I applaud these forward thinkers. These guys get it, they saw a need, and they selected the best candidate. I have not disappointed them nor have I let the community down. I stand for what's right, even if it is not popular.

I promised my mother and my family that I would serve with respect for my family and respect for those that helped me along the way. I still have that respect.

My mother passed in 2011. I was crushed, but I know she fought a good fight and finished her course. She rests in heaven with our Heavenly Father.

I have to tell this story on how some folks on this job don't get it. When my dear mother passed, I was hurt, crushed and notified my valley command staff. They sent out a Department Wide Notice. "We regret to announce the death of Odessa Brox, mother of Detective III Michael Brox, Serial No. 23333. The Chief of Police (not the black one) sent me a card of condolences; it seemed like hundreds of police officers, detectives, sergeants and command staff sent cards and emails expressing their heartfelt condolences.

The Los Angeles Police Protective League came to my mother's house and shared their support. LAPWOA (a women's police organization) sent their condolences. La Lay (the Hispanic Officers Organization) did the same. Family and friends from near and far to give a word of comfort and prayer.

Shortly after my mother's service, I received an email from OJB (a black police officers association) inviting me to a party and barbecue. This uncaring, backstabbing good for nothing, non-accountable, money stealing, money wasting group never even lifted a finger to type a former twenty-year member of the organization a short email in response to my mother's death, yet they had the nerve and tackiness to send me a party flyer.

Black folks! Get the fuck outta here!

I confronted them on the issue. Their excuse, "We had no idea, we did not know." Typical bullshit; the department created a death and funeral notice for my mother. "Nigga, please!"

By the time I made Detective III, I was a seasoned veteran. This was strange when these young folks were calling me "Sir." That was a trip. Then, what really brought it home was that some of my employees were older than I was, yet had less time on. They called me "Boss."

Devonshire was a good place to work. After a more senior Detective II left, I was the most senior employee and the only black supervising detective sergeant in entire command.

I worked hard, the lieutenant that hired me, first assigned me to supervise the detectives working auto theft cases. Then he moved me to my forté, Sex Crimes Investigations.

I had a good crew of investigators working for me. They were young, sarcastic (I like that) and wanted to serve. We were turning some good cases and serving the community well. My boss added more responsibility to me. Supervise the Major Assault Unit. This unit included a very knowledgeable Detective I. He had worked for me before at West Valley. He was one of my nighttime J Car officers. So I trusted him due to his experience and time on the job. I had a civilian who was very polite, funny and worked hard. She gave balance to the MAC unit. My Detective II, he was a piece of work, a very nice guy with a limited vocabulary. It seems like every other word out of his mouth was "fuckin'." Even describing a great dinner, a dental appointment and church service was described with that word. I spoke to him at least three times regarding his language in the squad room. He was so used to using the word; he did not know he was using it. I wrote a comment card to get his attention. That did not go over very well. He considered himself to be one of the vocal leaders at Devonshire. However, he was slacking on his productivity. His work suffered due to him being a rebel rouser amongst a small group of uninspired P2s who worked the juvenile unit.

This was a challenge. A great guy, a bit of a sour puss but overall a good guy. I kind of backed off and allowed him to make the changes gradually. That seemed to work until I conducted an audit on his and others work.

He was extremely behind with his suspected elder abuse cases. I let my new boss know. He was a lying, backstabbing racist. He first told me that I could handle the backlog without any further involvement from his office.

I instructed my Detective II that he needed to buckle down and serve this segment of our community with as much passion as he gives to rousing the troops on the lack of leadership on the department. The next thing I know, my new boss told me he was moving me off the Sex Crimes Unit. His excuse, "I need you to show me that you are capable of running a table, so were going to start you off at the auto table." Wait a minute, the most senior person at the division, a Detective III who has worked ALL OVER THIS CITY.

My sex unit employees carried the highest clearance rate in the entire Valley and third highest in the ENTIRE CITY.

No explanation was given, I put in for a transfer. I was not going to wait around and go through what I did at CTD again. I found out that when he got the position in detectives, He made a promise to a Detective II that SHE (a young female Detective II) would work and eventually run HIS Sex Crimes Unit. So I did what anyone with my time on would do. I asked him straight up if he had plans for someone else to run Sex, he said, "No."

"Okay, I still gotta go," I said, and I did.

Less than a week after I left, my chair still spinning from the vortex of my departure, a new young female detective II was running the table. Shortly thereafter, she was promoted to detective III. Hey lieutenant, you are a lying SOB.

CHAPTER NINE

Corruption

The LAPD has experienced its share of corrupt police officers and administrators for a number of years. Several books and stories made into movies have been introduced to the public and the world.

However, there is still a segment of active and on-going corruption within the walls of the LAPD. Corruption against its own rank and file and to the public we are sworn to "Protect and Serve."

I eluded to some of the deeds that go on as a daily routine. Employees (police officers and lower level supervisors) are forced, by threats of termination and future employment of any other Law Enforcement agency, to "buy into" the acts and misdeeds by upper command staff and the office of the Chief of Police.

As an example of corruption, The Christopher Dorner incident was blanketed with corruption that was given directly to the public, but things that were not sensational or the "big story" was swept over by this agency.

Let me be perfectly clear, I DO NOT condone or support Dorner's actions. He was wrong to do the things he was accused of doing. Murder is not an acceptable action for anger and frustration. I will be the first in line to drop the lever on a cold-blooded killer of innocent men, women and children.

However, if one would ask, "What happened to the officers and their sergeants, who were scared out of their boots in Torrance at the sound of newspapers being delivered in a quiet community and with no other information, fired over one hundred rounds without a target or credible threat?" the answers would be evasive and non-committal. The officers and sergeants are still working the streets and considered heroes. They violated every single policy of the use of force and the shooting policy. However, the corrupt upper echelon of this department swept this under the rug.

The Chief of Police turned the use of color into a sideshow. He and his command staff formulated a plan to deceive the public and discredit ALL black officers that have cried out to his position in hopes to get relief from being discriminated against. He used a very dark skinned female sergeant to go on national TV to speak for those that have been silenced by the corrupt internal investigation system and those that are still struggling to hold on despite being treated unfairly.

Is the community safe? Our former chief from New York came to Los Angeles in hopes to make a change after the Consent Decree pointed out a number of problematic organizational ways in which LAPD was doing business.

This thing called COMPSTAT was designed to hold police managers accountable, specifically geographic patrol divisions. This has turned into a numbers game. EACH WEEK, most or all of the twenty-one geographic patrol divisions within LAPD hold what they referred to as a "crime control" meeting. The name is nowhere near what actually goes on behind doors. It has little or nothing to do with community safety.

Numbers and Stats

The LAPD, the Chief and the Mayor want the community members of Los Angeles to believe that crime is down. This is nothing but smoke, posturing, lies and deception. The corruption lies in this system of COMPSTAT.

Born out of the New York Police Department model brought to you by former NYPD Commissioner, each division has a group of computer nerds, geeks that do a bunch of work with numbers and stats. The unit is called Crime Analysis Detail. They are not held accountable to provide detailed information about crime. However, they really picked apart reported crime to find a loophole to change the national crime coding to make it appear that crime is actually down.

For example, crime is broken into Part I and Part II. More serious crimes of violence are considered Part I along with burglary, robbery and crimes against women. Those stats are reported nationally and later made public.

I have been responsible for auto theft, robberies, major assault crimes and sexual assault. Here is where the corruption comes in.

People want to feel safe and secure in their homes and with their possessions.

Car theft and Car Burglaries

I recently had a couple of apartment complexes with hundreds of residents who live on the same street and within a few blocks of each other. Several of the residents had their vehicles broken into or things taken from unlocked cars.

Our crime analysis details computer geeks, at the direction of the commanding officer, at the demand of the bureau chief to please the chief and the mayor came to my desk and insisted that we make ALL of these crimes into a single incident. How?

Well, the national uniform reporting guideline allows in its description that property crimes committed at the same time by the same suspects and the same location may be considered one incident. The key word is MAY.

So it was ordered that all the crime report numbers be canceled except one. That one report will have all the names of the victims that had their property stolen. So it would appear to the unsuspecting public that one person's vehicle was broken into not the 34 that was initially reported. So when the stats are published, it gives the impression that crime is down. This is the same with residential and Business Burglary. If multiple structures are broken into during the above-described manner, it will be changed into one incident. Thus, it looks like only one burglary took place. This practice drives the number down.

Lies and Deceptions

Recently in a crime control meeting, I witness the back and forth banter between a detective and the command officer of the division. There were about five people in a car and suspects shot at and into the car. One person was hit and all were named victims' of Assault with a Deadly Weapon. He was ordered to make only one victim, cancel the report for the others and make them witnesses.

This information, if (it is) practiced throughout the city, multiplied over and over again during a calendar year, crime stats would drastically drop. But the public is being lied to and the stats are not being reported accurately. Corruption.

Another form of corruption is FAVOR. It has been noticed that if you have favor, you can accomplish much. The Chief of Police has the final say on ALL internal matters involving his employees and their conduct, promotions and assignments.

Examples

An unknown young black police officer with a short time on the job is involved in a domestic incident at his home and another police agency arrives. The LAPD officer is inside his home, obviously intoxicated. There was no crime, just an argument between him and his girlfriend. Some neighbor called the local PD. They notified the LAPD that one of their employees was intoxicated during their investigation.

LAPD does an "INVESTIGATION" and forces him to sign a lifetime "no alcohol" contract, months later he is beaten to a pulp at a restaurant with his wife and family by local gang members. He told the responding officers he had a beer or two, LAPD, with the chief's approval, fired him for violating the contract. No favor!

Another young LAPD officer, the nephew of a well-known and respected former commander and former commanding officer of LAPD's "elite" Metro Division. This young officer was off duty in another city, at a nightclub. Angry that some other men were flirting with his girlfriend. This young officer, very intoxicated created a disturbance enough so that local PD had to be called. He was belligerent, cursing, called a black security officer "monkey and nigger." It was reported that this drunken officer also was waving his firearm around and making threats.

He was arrested and booked by the responding agency. He had his LAPD Internal Board of Rights. It was recommended that this young embarrassment of an officer be fired. However, because of FAVOR, the Chief of Police reinstated this officer and gave him a suspension for a few days. This officer is in uniform and may be patrolling your neighborhood. FAVOR! Forgot to mention, this officer is WHITE.

The Chief's daughter—an LAPD officer working Metro Division's Elite Mounted Unit owned and cared for her horse— paid for horse feed, grooming, tack and to be shod. She figured how about I ride my own horse at work. She sold her horse to the city of Los Angeles (citizens paid for this) and received money in her pocket. Now her own horse is being fed and the above by the city of Los Angeles. The Chief of Police approved this transaction. He was questioned about the issue and LIED. He claimed he did not notice the documents and check he approved was his daughter and her horse. I surmise that anyone else should sell their car to the city, drive it to and from work using city gas and maintenance. Sounds fair to me! Favor, she has not been ordered or told to return the money—almost $10, 000. She still will not ride the horse designated for her to use. She rides HER horse.

These examples and other hundreds of cases are clearly corrupt. Corruption and favor caused a ripple effect in the way LAPD does and does not serve the communities of Los Angeles.

CHAPTER TEN

Sworn Employees

This is the city of Los Angeles, a city of so many different ethnic groups, religious beliefs, cultures and monetary wealth and poverty.

The majority of white police officers on the LAPD Do Not live in or near the city of Los Angeles. Most of them live in the far reaches of the county of Los Angeles.

People (police officers included) tend to have a vested interest and care for their surroundings. People most likely live, shop and raised their children in familiar areas, surrounded by people that they have a similar interest in.

A lot of officers, white officers don't care about the city or its people. They have openly said that they are only here for the money. The evidence is in the numbers. How many white officers actually live in the city of Los Angeles?

I saw a couple of uniformed officers driving on a very populated street. A "hot call" was broadcast; these officers tossed out bags of fast food onto the street and proceeded to respond to the call.

It is a problem when many of the white officers or any officer publicly expresses his or her personal opinion on politics or religion. That is very dangerous as a public servant. Countless officers openly blame our president for the number of attacks on police officers nationwide. They absolutely refuse to acknowledge that these crimes, which disgust us all are the responsibility of criminals with long criminal backgrounds. Yet, in years past under other presidents, when officers were killed in the line of duty or attacked,   none of the police officers I know and came across before 2008 blamed attacks and deaths of officers on prior Presidents. Racism is alive and well inside the LAPD.

Black officers are afraid of their own shadows. Some even cower at the thought that they will not be able to promote or loose FAVOR. A number of black officers have lost their way. Some have forgotten where they and their families came from. A large number of us knew it took a village to get us on this police department, but once we were hired, we don't give back. We failed to reach out and help those of us that needed support, needed a shoulder to cry on or a word of encouragement when things were tough.

As I'm writing this book, LAPD is struggling to hire black applicants. I have personal knowledge of four applicants that were uniquely qualified to become a member of this agency. All four were female and black. None were hired. Three of the four were hired by other police agencies; the other is in Law School. There are many more recent stories of qualified black applicants that are being denied.

The problem with this information is that it is getting worse. The LAPD has only five black probationary officers going through training. There are three academy classes being trained now, of those classes there are only two black recruits.

There is a massive number of black officers, detectives, and sergeants who were hired in the early eighties and nineties who are leaving LAPD due to retirements in the next three years. Soon, many Los Angeles residences in the black communities will not see a brother or sister in uniform.

Recruitment is not actively seeking black officers. The only black organization we have is standing still (moving only at parties, dinners and barbecues). The OJB has the potential to visit all the Los Angeles universities, colleges, trade schools, high and middle schools to introduce this career to interested young people of color. Our communities are screaming for it. But this organization is not listening or afraid how it would look, trying and making an effort to bring in our own. Many young Los Angeles people have an image of LAPD; we can change it, one person at a time.

CHAPTER ELEVEN

The Pot and the Kettle

LAPD officers have traditionally stood firm on the ideas of brotherhood before community, officer's safety before reverence for the life of others and our house is cleaner than yours.

During training or "street survival" (which I am not opposed to the concept), it is drilled into the young minds of impressionable officers to trust no one. Trust only those in blue. That logic, although well intended, has created this "holier than thou" mentality. Officers from the LAPD have often referred to members of the community as "those people," "ass holes" and many other degrading names and titles.

The first glimpse into these mindsets and secret conversations were revealed and illustrated during the "Rodney King era." The names officers used to describe members of different ethnic groups and cultures were shocking, to say the least, yet it explained a portion of the divide between the police and our community.

What was—and still is—interesting was that some of the officers making these demeaning comments were raised and educated in the same communities they now cursed.

During a conversation with an informal group of officers standing around the Foothill desk, regarding the east San Fernando Valley, a young Hispanic officer exclaimed, "All these people around here are fucking assholes!" I found his statement to be self-degrading. I validated this by his own previous conversation that he revealed that he grew up in Pacoima and his family still lived in the same community and house that gave him his start in life in the exact same community that he grouped as assholes.

So the people in his family were assholes? His mother, father, his sisters, brothers, and grandparents? He now lives in Lilly white Santa Clarita with his blended family. This officer has lost touch with reality. The reality that geography has little or nothing to do with a person's love of life and others.

Scores of LAPD officers have the same mentality. Black officers have adopted the "pot calling the kettle black" mind-set. Repressing childhood memories of where they grew up and the struggles of today's families. Officers will look at broken down cars and graffiti on walls and buildings, and shake their heads, verbally question, and judge why or how people could live like this. Yet in the secured bathroom stall of countless police stations, one could read etchings of how hated a black Chief of Police is, how specific female officers, detectives and other ranks "suck dick" or "take it up the ass."

Most LAPD's men's locker rooms smelled of dirty socks, trash, and discarded dry cleaning plastic bags lined the floors. Hangers and dried shoe polish were on the floors, just a few steps away from a half-filled garbage can.

The urinals were filled with gum, rejected and chewed smokeless tobacco. The walls at these urinals often had dried mucus or spit plastered at eye level, the toilets seats were pee-stained, and the bowl was filled with unflushed human waste.

Senior and salty officers violated department policy by using chewing tobacco and used clear bottles to spit inside the often-clear containers. The nasty and discussing brown liquid trophies littered the stations and squad rooms.

The patrol cars were filled with cracked sunflower seeds, cups, and bags of half-eaten food. The vehicle doors were often offline due to officers using their foot to push the doors open, leaving boot prints, damaged armrests and bent hinges. Steering wheels with gaping sectional plugs, writing on the dashboards and ripped interior.

An LAPD's officer's personal behavior does not differ from that of those we served. After a domestic violence call and having been to the house before with the same couple., judgments start. "Why does she stay there?" "If I were in her shoes!"

The police officer profession has one of the highest rates of divorce. There are far too many incidents of domestic VIOLENCE between officers and their mates to condemn the community for nuptial discord.

Their blind allegiance to their political party has blinded them to ignore FACTS that the President has shown support for future retiring officers, injured officers and the death of officers in the line of duty nationwide. There has never been a past president that has attended funerals, called widows and signed legislature to show how human he is and how he feels. No one agrees with ALL things political but to ignore the FACT that this president has shown support is unthinkable.

There are "uncle toms" that have encouraged and participated in blatant disrespect of the president. Accepting ethnic racial slurs on their social media pages by people they call friends. I guess it is okay to call the first and only black president a "coon." Judgmental of the way "these people" live? Now that is, "The pot calling the kettle black."

CHAPTER TWELVE

Christopher Dorner Case

No further comment.

LAPD stationed officers at the homes of suspected targets of Dorner. The officers in Torrance were so scared; frightened that they shot over one hundred rounds into a vehicle they thought was being driven by Dorner. They reacted after they heard what they thought were gunshots and began indiscriminately and wildly firing at a truck. When the smoke cleared, they had fired upon two old ladies that were delivering newspapers in the community. Over one hundred rounds were fired into and at this vehicle. God must have been looking out for these innocent people (or LAPD officer can't shoot worth a shit) because they were not injured. Now LAPD has a shooting policy and simply because you are on a protective detail, the policy remains in effect.

They did not know their target (they guessed).

They emptied their weapons and reloaded and kept on shooting.

None of the officers were in a last resort situation.

None of the officers could have possible (without facts know to them at the time) knew that the use of deadly force was justified.

None of the officers considered the background in a residential community.

None of the officers saw a suspect (two small women).

Dorner was six feet plus, black and bald.

Yet after the shooting of these innocent women and the nearly deadly actions by the officers and a supervisor, none of the officers were suspended or fired.

They damn near killed two innocent women. FAVOR?

How does LAPD and the City restore Police and Community relations?

Media

Movies

Recruitment

Mutual respect

If you are from the community create

Mandatory residence within the City Limits

Police Science and Police Careers in Middle Schools

Mandatory weekly visits with elementary school students

Conclusion

My thirty-five years working for the LAPD has been bittersweet. I loved serving the people whom I served. I love and appreciate many of my co-workers. There are things I learned and became aware of while working for the police department that I could have only learned being in such an environment.

Being Black in Blue is not an easy task. Many times, you are not respected by your colleagues or the public whom you serve, especially non-blacks. However, when you do unto others as you would have them do unto you, and you treat every person with respect, you sleep well at night knowing you have done your very best and you have pleased God.

While I appreciate my partners in the field who had my back, I know for sure it was my mother's prayers and God Almighty who protected me. I would see the pride in the eyes of blacks when they would see Blacks in Blue. Our family, friends and the community had no idea about the attitudes, prejudices and racism among those who were our partners.

It's easier for those who join the force and choose to stay in their place. However, for the Black in Blue who choose to pursue higher positions they are more than qualified for—they can become mentally/emotionally broken for just trying to use their talent which would enhance the department.

The old adage, "The more things change, the more they stay the same" is a reality for the police department. I penned this book so that those who join the force to serve and protect might have an inside glimpse of what it is like to be Black in Blue. My message is not to deter you from wanting to serve and protect the community. When I say protect I am not just talking about protecting property but human beings.

We desperately need more Black men in Blue and I encourage you to become a part. Nevertheless, I want those who come aboard to have an understanding of the environment in which you will serve. I commit to you that knowing what you are stepping into prior to can serve you better.

I contend that I am a stronger man today because I overcame the obstacles that were placed in my path. Today, I am retired and living life on my terms, and I give God all the praise. For those who are a part of the corruption, prejudice, and racism, I hope you will find the book as a mirror to view your attitude and reflect on the lives and families you may have destroyed unknowingly. May you change now, so that the future will be brighter and lighter for the next generations.

About the Author

Michael Anthony Brox was born June 10, 1960 in Los Angeles, California. He is the sixth of seven children born to Grady Brox, Jr. and Odessa Brox.

The family lived in rented housing in the area of Santa Barbara Boulevard and Central Avenue, and later, on Slauson Avenue near Normandie Avenue. After a fire at the home near Normandie, Michael's family moved to the Pueblo Housing Projects on the Eastside of Los Angeles. There, his family consisted of their mother and father and six kids, who occupied a two-bedroom project unit near Holmes Ave School.

Young Michael enjoyed playing in a nearby lumberyard, jumping on pallets of wood, and running from the lumberyard's security and junkyard dogs as forms of excitement. The memories of financial struggles that often left him and his brother and sisters with what he now know were meals just to keep them fed; rice and butter, sugar bread, and powered milk, which seemed like the real thing. At times, that was all the family had to eat.

Clothes were often handed down, either given to us, or purchased from rummage stores. The clothes were clean, and used, but we stayed warm, and Mom kept us looking like millions.

Watching the Watts riots unfold, seemingly right in front of our project building, was confusing and exciting to the eyes of young Michael. Seeing "Army Men" holding rifles, walking in the streets followed by tanks and jeeps, stirred this young mind.

Finally, the family moved to Gardena, California, in 1968.

After our parents separated, Mom struggled as a single parent, now with seven children.

I learned my work ethic from watching my mother work in the LA Unified School District, and sell items at swap meets and second hand stores on the side. She hustled to feed her children.

To help out, I started throwing newspapers for two different papers. My mother would help me on Sundays because I started so early, and the papers were extremely heavy. I worked summer jobs for the City of Gardena, which included cleaning up vacant lots, or the yards of struggling seniors, and the removal of trash from the vacant buildings.

Later, I worked for a rental car company and bagged groceries for a supermarket. During the same time, I was going to High school and later onto college.

Education all over Los Angeles:
Hooper Ave School
135th Street Elementary School
Henry Clay Jr High School
Gardena High School
Los Angeles Harbor College

My career at the Los Angeles Police Department
1981 - 2016
Police Officer II
Police Officer III
Detective I
Detective II
Detective III